RESOURCE BOOKS FOR TEACHERS

series editor
ALAN MALEY

DRAMA

Charlyn Wessels

Oxford University Press

Oxford University Press
Walton Street, Oxford OX2 6DP

Oxford New York
Athens Auckland Bangkok Bombay
Calcutta Cape Town Dar es Salaam Delhi
Florence Hong Kong Istanbul Karachi
Kuala Lumpur Madras Madrid Melbourne
Mexico City Nairobi Paris Singapore
Taipei Tokyo Toronto
and associated companies in
Berlin Ibadan

Oxford and *Oxford English* are trade marks of
Oxford University Press

ISBN 0 19 437097 6

© Oxford University Press 1987

First published 1987
Sixth impression 1994

Set by Katerprint Typesetting Services, Oxford

Printed in Hong Kong

Acknowledgements

We thank the writers and publishers who have allowed us to use texts that fall within their copyright:

Woody Allen for an extract from *Play It Again, Sam*; David Campton for an extract from 'Us and Them' (in *Double Act*, edited by Mark Shackleton, published by Edward Arnold, 1985); Doug Case and Ken Wilson for 'The Ticket Inspector' (from *Off-Stage! Sketches from the English Teaching Theatre*, published by Heinemann Educational Books, 1979); the estate of Agatha Christie for an extract from 'The Patient' (from *Twenty One-Act Plays*, edited by Stanley Richards, published by Samuel French, 1978); John Eastwood, Valerie Kay, Ronald Mackin, and Peter Strevens for an extract from *Network 1 Student's Book* (published by Oxford University Press, 1980); Herb Gardner for an extract from *Thieves*; T. C. Jupp, John Milne, Philip Prowse, and Judy Garton-Springer for an extract from *Encounters Student's Book* (published by Heinemann Educational Books, 1979); the Literary Trustees of Walter de la Mare and the Society of Authors for 'The Listeners'; the estate of Carl Sandburg for 'Sea Chest' from *Good Morning, America* (published by Harcourt Brace Jovanovich, 1916); P. L. Sandler and C. L. Stott for an extract from *Manage with English* (published by Oxford University Press, 1981); Peter Shaffer for an extract from 'The Private Ear' (from *Four Plays* by Peter Shaffer, published by Penguin Books, 1981); Renée Taylor and Joseph Bologna for an extract from *Lovers and Other Strangers*; John Turner and the Circus of Poets for '1-2-3-4' and 'Chewing Chestnuts' (from *OK Gimme – Poems for Children*, published by Versewagon Press) and 'Hey Look At Me' (from *Hard Shoulders Second Home*, published by Versewagon Press); the estate of Tennessee Williams for an extract from *A Streetcar Named Desire*.

Contents

The author and series editor

Charlyn Wessels taught English as a Second Language in a South African secondary school before working as a lecturer in a teacher training college in Cape Town for three years. On moving to Europe, she taught EFL at the Free University of West Berlin, and spent four years as a tutor at the Institute for Applied Language Studies at the University of Edinburgh, where she started one of the first Drama for TEFL courses, which is still running successfully each year during the Edinburgh Festival. She then lectured for six years at Stevenson College, Edinburgh, where she also started a range of English through Drama courses. During this period, she ran many workshops in drama for teachers' groups in the UK and Europe. She has been acting 'since the age of three', and has long experience of producing plays with amateur actors. Since her return to South Africa, she has been lecturing at the University of the Western Cape, where she co-ordinates that university's academic literacy programme. Together with her English through Drama students, she has written two readers for the MacMillan Bookshelf series, *Soap Opera*, and *Soap Two—The Sequel*. She was also a contributing author to the *Pilgrims English Course*, Books 1 and 2, published in Spain by Equipo SM (1990), and regularly publishes articles or contributes to books on Drama and Pronunciation.

Alan Maley worked for The British Council from 1962 to 1988, serving as English Language Officer in Yugoslavia, Ghana, Italy, France, and China, and as Regional Representative in South India (Madras). From 1988 to 1993 he was Director-General of the Bell Educational Trust, Cambridge. He is currently Senior Fellow in the Department of English Language and Literature of the National University of Singapore. He has written *Literature*, in this series, *Beyond Words, Sounds Interesting, Sounds Intriguing, Words, Variations on a Theme,* and *Drama Techniques in Language Learning* (all with Alan Duff), *The Mind's Eye* (with Françoise Grellet and Alan Duff), and *Learning to Listen* and *Poem into Poem* (with Sandra Moulding). He is also Series Editor for the New Perspectives and Oxford Supplementary Skills series.

Foreword

The value of drama techniques for language learning has steadily risen on the Communicative Stock Exchange over the past ten years. Drama is now readily accepted alongside simulations, information-gap activities, problem-solving, and the like, in a way which would previously have been inconceivable.

There is, however, no room for complacency. All too often, acceptance of an approach does not guarantee its implementation. In fact it may be a form of resistance to it. Or it may lead to merely nominal changes, whereby old habits are given new names.

This book comes then as a salutary reminder of the need to justify the use of drama, and to continue to explore its possibilities in the EFL classroom. It moves on from the pioneering work of writers in the early 1980s in two significant directions:

- by seeking to incorporate drama into the workaday areas of coursebook dialogues and texts, and pronunciation teaching;
- by using drama to illuminate texts, and in particular literary texts, and by moving outside the classroom through drama projects.

At the same time it diversifies the range of improvisation and drama game activities initiated in earlier work.

It is a most welcome addition to the literature in this area, and will become an essential text for teachers and teacher trainers who start to explore its rich possibilities.

Alan Maley

Preface

This book is intended for in-service native and non-native teachers of English as a Foreign or Second Language. It aims to demystify drama and show how it can be introduced into everyday lessons, and how it can be used as an extra-curricular activity.

The Introduction will set out the theoretical background of drama in language teaching and the rationale for using it not just in language learning, but in all learning. The rest of the book is divided into two sections. In Section One, the focus of interest is on drama as a supplementary technique of communicative language teaching in the following areas:

- spoken communication skills;
- improving coursebook presentation;
- improving pronunciation and other prosodic features;
- the teaching of literature – improving students' understanding of text (simplified and unsimplified).

Section Two focuses on the drama project: it assesses its place and value in language teaching, and offers practical advice on setting up a project with a group of learners.

Chapter 1 sets out the essential components of a lesson using drama. It considers how to introduce drama techniques to students who have never experienced them before and may be hostile towards something they may regard as frivolous and time-consuming. The chapter will focus on the creation of the right atmosphere, the role of the teacher, the role of the most co-operative students, and the need for careful planning, timing, and preparation in lessons using drama.

Chapter 2, entitled 'Drama games', contains forty short games, both verbal and non-verbal, which can be used in a variety of ways. Some of these are suitable for use at the beginning of a lesson, while others can be used to round off a lesson or a particular activity. Their function is to prepare for, to revise, or to reinforce taught material.

Chapter 3 concentrates on improving basic coursebook presentation. It examines the ways in which dialogues, role plays, and simulations are commonly presented, and considers how drama can be used to improve the teaching of these and other techniques. Sample lessons are given to demonstrate how drama can be included in coursebook presentation.

In **Chapter 4**, we consider how the techniques used by actors to prepare their voices for the stage can be transferred to the language-teaching classroom – techniques such as vocal warm-ups, chants, singing, tongue-twisters, and choral reading. A selection of techniques that have proved successful with learners is presented, together with advice on the selection and preparation of materials suitable for the teaching of pronunciation, intonation, and other prosodic features.

Chapter 5 covers an area broadly described as 'the spoken communication skills'. It looks at the use of drama in what are normally considered as 'afternoon activities' – dramatized playreadings, improvisations, role plays, and video-discussion lessons. It includes a number of scenes from the works of such well-known playwrights as Woody Allen and Peter Shaffer.

In the final chapter of Section One, the focus is on drama in the teaching of literature – and here I must acknowledge the work of Dorothy Heathcote on teaching text through drama. It is principally as a result of her inspiration and example that many of the ideas in this chapter have come to fruition.

The three chapters of Section Two concern the drama project. They assess its place and value in language teaching, and offer practical advice on setting up a project, and the management of rehearsals. These chapters are based on my four drama projects carried out with EFL students of different nationalities and levels, at the Institute for Applied Language Studies, University of Edinburgh.

Most of the lessons presented in the book have been previously tested, and the methods they employ can be applied quite easily to other lessons. None of them is presented as a finished product. Teachers should feel free to experiment, to introduce variations of these lessons, or add more spice to the basic mixture as they see fit.

Introduction

I hear and I forget,
I listen and I remember,
I do and I understand.
(Chinese proverb)

What is drama?

Drama is doing. Drama is being. Drama is such a normal thing. It is something that we all engage in daily when faced with difficult situations. You get up in the morning with a bad headache or an attack of depression, yet you face the day and cope with other people, pretending that nothing is wrong. You have an important meeting or an interview coming up, so you 'talk through' the issues with yourself beforehand and decide how to present a confident, cheerful face, what to wear, what to do with your hands, and so on. You've spilt coffee over a colleague's papers, and immediately you prepare an elaborate excuse. Your partner has just run off with your best friend, yet you cannot avoid going in to teach a class of inquisitive students. Getting on with our day-to-day lives requires a series of civilized masks if we are to maintain our dignity and live in harmony with others. For, as Shakespeare said:

All the world's a stage
and all the men and women merely players.
(*As You Like It*)

In the four scenarios I have just described, the following elements were all present:

- situation, problem, solution: surface reality
- background, emotions, planning: underlying reality/foundation.

In learning anything, all six of these elements have to be present for that which is learned to be fully acquired and retained. To give an example: if a learner of English asked you 'What is a blind person?', you might simply reply, 'A blind person cannot see', and this would probably satisfy him intellectually. But if you replied, 'Shut your eyes and try to find your pen on the desk in front of you', you would be involving him in the actual experience of being blind, and would thus satisfy him not only intellectually, but emotionally as well, and possibly inspire in him feelings of empathy with all blind people. He would be more likely to remember the meaning of the word as a result of this moment of direct experience. This is what Brian Way, in his book *Development Through Drama*, calls the 'precise' function of drama.

And yet, in so much of our teaching, we fail to realize the importance of providing our students with direct experience. We present them with only the surface reality and then wonder why they forget the lessons so easily. But the direct experience that drama offers can encompass both realities.

Drama is what happens when we allow our students to explore the foundations of the surface reality. When we give them the background to a situation, or allow them to guess at it, we deepen their perceptions of the situation. When we ask, 'How do you think he/she feels at this moment? How would *you* feel? What is he/she thinking?', we unlock learners' own feelings of empathy with the person or situation being studied. When we ask them to improvise a continuation of a story, to supply an introduction, or to offer alternative conclusions, we are stimulating their imaginations and their intellects. And when, finally, we ask students to 'get up and do it', we are rewarding their efforts with our interest and attention, and their enjoyment of the *doing* (for the most basic reward of drama is that it is fun to do) is the final consolidator.

The view of drama in the classroom as learning through direct experience (both our own and that of others) means that drama cannot be restricted only to certain areas of the language-teaching curriculum. At any moment in our teaching we can be confronted with situations where words fail, and only action can help the learners to understand.

Drama in education uses the same tools employed by actors in the theatre. In particular, it uses improvisation and mime. But while in the theatre everything is contrived for the benefit of the audience, in classroom drama everything is contrived for the benefit of the learners.

Where does drama fit into language teaching?

Drama is not, like communicative language teaching, a new *theory* of language teaching, but rather a *technique* which can be used to develop certain language skills. Currently many teachers view it simply as something enjoyable (but fraught with dangers and difficulties), to be used mainly with easy-going, extrovert students during classes in spoken communication skills. The result is that many teachers tend to steer clear of it. But there are others, such as Gavin Bolton, who take the opposite view: that drama should be placed at the centre of the curriculum, applicable to all aspects of learning. I would prefer to take the middle course: drama is neither a terrifying, riderless horse to be approached only by the naturally extrovert, nor is it a complete answer to all the problems of language teaching.

There are at least four areas of the weekly language-teaching timetable where drama can be used effectively.

Teaching the coursebook

First of all, there is the session generally known as the 'coursebook slot'. Most language-teaching coursebooks already use, or attempt to use, drama techniques to some extent. They contain dialogues, role plays, simulations, games, and songs. Learners enjoy doing these activities in groups or pairs, and the most enjoyable activities are frequently the ones best remembered and learnt. There is scope within each of these for the application of drama techniques such as improvisation, mime, character analysis, observation, interpretation, and invention to help learners in their acquisition of the language.

Teaching the four skills

Secondly, there is the session referred to as the 'skills slot' – individual lessons focusing on the improvement of each of the four skills (reading, writing, speaking/pronunciation, and listening). Drama has a role to play in each of these, but particularly in the acquisition of correct pronunciation, rhythm, intonation, and other prosodic features. We can learn a lot from considering the ways in which actors prepare their voices for the stage. Vocal warm-ups, chanting, choral speaking, and singing are only a few of the techniques that could help learners to improve pronunciation and prosody.

Teaching spoken communication skills

Thirdly, there are the lessons in 'spoken communication skills', and here the role of drama is obvious in getting students to speak. Drama can generate a *need to speak* by focusing the attention of the learners on creating a drama, dialogue, or role play, or solving a problem (as in simulations and games). These lessons are commonly used as 'afternoon activities', with the emphasis on production rather than reception. They include discussions, debates, role plays, simulations, games, prepared talks, and even dramatized play readings. In each of these activities, learners have to be active participants, using their imagination and interacting with each other; almost unconsciously they are acquiring communication skills in the foreign language.

And yet, so often, these lessons are dull and pedestrian, inspiring only the minimum of communication, with the teacher supplying most of the language needed. The fault here lies not with the materials, but with the preparation of the students, the group dynamics in the class, and the presentation by the teacher. We cannot expect our students to perform adequately by simply assigning them roles or functions and telling them to 'get on with it'. We need to take account of social and psychological factors that are conducive to creating an atmosphere of relaxation, trust, and mutual co-operation, in which the learner feels confident and happy enough to assume a different role or persona.

The drama project

So far, we have concentrated on drama in the classroom. But the drama project which leads to the full-scale staging of a play in the target language can provide a particularly satisfying experience for learners. Working on such a long-term project, learning lines, and constantly using the target language during rehearsals, becoming part of a coherent unit and growing in confidence with each rehearsal, are all likely to increase the learner's competence in the target language. It does, however, have some disadvantages:

- It can be used effectively only with small groups of volunteer students.
- Not all students will perceive it as being inherently useful, and so will fail to bring with them the high degree of 'motivational readiness' essential for the success of such a project.
- It is time-intensive, requiring considerable planning and organizational skills from the teacher, and dedication and loyalty from the students.

Of course, if one is dealing with trainee teachers, it is easy to convince them that drama is a valid component of their training; but it is difficult to convince serious post-graduate or academically-orientated students of the value of the project. The only thing that will attract them is the success of the project, and the rapid progress made in the target language by those students who have volunteered for it.

The teacher who embarks on a project with learners of a language should not hope to achieve anything of great artistic or theatrical merit. The reward will lie in the greater confidence and ability of the students to use the target language. In Section Two we shall look at the project in more detail to assess its value and potential.

It will be seen, then, that drama is a marvellously flexible technique that can fit into any area of the timetable. It requires no major adjustments on the part of the teacher. It does not even demand that teachers should change the materials they are presenting. But it will help to bring the materials to life, by infusing the lifeless print with the feelings, imaginations, and thoughts of the learners, who become active participants in the learning process.

What can drama achieve?

In language teaching, drama should be viewed as a technique of communicative language teaching. This is currently the dominant theory of language teaching. It emphasizes the role of the learner as active participant rather than passive receptor. The greatest problem with this theory is that it is often difficult to link it to practice. Numerous 'communicative' coursebooks have been written, full of wonderful ideas and methods, yet many teachers still find it difficult to achieve the ideals of these books in the classroom. Do these books, and the methods they present, actually teach *genuine* communication, or do they condemn both learner and teacher to artificial and contrived dialogues? To answer this question, we need to consider what we mean by 'genuine communication'.

Genuine communication, first of all, involves speaking to another person, but not in the tidy A/B/A/B sequence that we see in typical coursebook dialogues. Most ordinary conversations contain hesitations, interruptions, distractions, misunderstandings, and even silences. Secondly, our emotions are involved. Depending on the subject, a conversation could evoke the whole spectrum of feelings from violent anger to tenderest love in the speakers – are they total strangers, friends, relatives, lovers, officials, or student and teacher? Relationships in turn will be affected by the status of each individual speaking. Is A a superior, and B her subordinate? Or does A merely *think* she is? And how will she address B in order to gain this superiority? Is B aware of A's deception? The status of each speaker can also be linked to the environment in which the conversation takes place. The lofty customs officer at the airport undergoes a radical change of status when stopped for speeding by the traffic police on the motorway. And finally, there is 'body language' – facial expressions, gestures, the positions of our limbs, and non-verbal sounds, which can be as eloquent as words. We know when people like us if they lean towards us when they speak to us, open their arms, and generally look 'approachable'. We find it difficult to speak to someone who never meets our eyes, shuffles about, or whose whole body says 'Keep off!'. As for non-verbal sounds, one whole side of a telephone conversation can be carried on with a series of grunts, *oohs*, and *aaarghs*!

Many of these aspects of 'genuine communication' are overlooked in much classroom practice or coursebook presentation, so it is hardly surprising that so many students fail, or take such a long time, to achieve the ability to communicate effectively outside the classroom.

A possible solution might be to write coursebook dialogues like plays, complete with stage directions, feelings expressed, gestures, and so on, and also to use much longer dialogues like the ones in Hartley and Viney's *Streamline* series. But until this happens, drama techniques can offer the committed and enthusiastic teacher a means of bringing classroom interaction to life. The use of drama would involve a consideration of most (if not all) of the aspects of genuine communication discussed earlier – background, emotions, relationships, status, body language, and other paralinguistic features.

But drama can offer much more than just the acquisition of a
genuine communicative ability. As Maley and Duff (*Drama
Techniques in Language Learning*) have so clearly demonstrated, it
can also be used to teach structure and vocabulary, and is an
effective technique for revision and reinforcement. To give a simple
example, verbs and the contexts in which they occur can be taught
and revised through mime. Using improvisation, original dialogues
can be created from a basic 'situational' vocabulary list, for example
'The Station'. Questions can be taught and revised through a
multitude of games like 'Who am I?', 'Any Questions?', and 'Find
your Partner' (see Chapter 2).

At the other end of the scale, there is the drama project, which is a
communicative activity on two levels: there is the level of learning
lines for a play, and rehearsing these – a formal type of learning by
the student volunteer; and there is the level of working on a project
for a set period within a group of students, which involves constant
discussion and interaction in the target language – an informal type
of natural acquisition, as opposed to conscious learning. It is this
second type of activity that I would like to discuss in more detail.

In this activity, the student is engaged in the creation of a dramatic
production – a self-chosen communicative activity in the genuine
sense. All forms of interaction take place in the target language, if it
is a mixed-nationality group. While it is potentially inhibiting to
insist on this rigidly with a monolingual group, it should be
encouraged as far as possible during rehearsals and discussions of
the production. If this can be achieved, most of the language
acquired during a drama project will probably stem not from the
actual play itself, but from the discussions surrounding the
production and the rehearsals. The student is learning, albeit
unintentionally. Frank Dunlop (1977) writes:

> . . . the passive side of learning is itself highly important since a
> great deal of what is ever learnt is unspecifiable, and hence has to
> be picked up or acquired at a less than fully conscious level.

In his book *Principles and Practice in Second Language Acquisition*,
Stephen Krashen distinguishes between the two types of learning
outlined above, and calls them 'acquisition' and 'learning'. He
writes:

> Language *acquisition* . . . requires meaningful interaction in the
> target language – natural communication – in which speakers are
> concerned not with the *form* of their utterances but with the
> *message* they are conveying and understanding.

> Conscious language *learning*, on the other hand, is thought to be
> helped a great deal by error correction and the presentation of
> explicit rules.

> In general, utterances are initiated by the acquired system – our
> fluency in production is based on what we have 'picked up'
> through active communication.

Discussing and planning the different stages in the drama project satisfies this principle through focusing not on form but on communication and meaning. This should be the central aim of all communicative language teaching, but it is rarely achieved. Possibly one of the most significant aspects of the drama project is this unconscious learning in a natural, uncontrived manner. The same type of acquisition happens, though on a smaller scale, in a group of students discussing a simulation or planning a role play.

Finally, I think it is true that students benefit psychologically from their involvement in a drama project. Rehearsing and performing a play in a target language improves the students' sense of confidence and self-esteem as learners, and this in its turn should increase their motivation with respect to acquiring the target language. Richard Via, one of the pioneers of drama in language teaching, writes about this psychological spin-off in an article entitled 'English through drama' (1972):

> We get involved with putting on a play rather than with the task of learning English, and so we do what everyone who teaches English really hopes to do – that is, to have the students learn by doing. We have fun, and the students learn by doing. We have fun, and the students will get great joy out of performing, and the audience, even the mothers and fathers who don't speak English, will be happy and delighted to see the performance. You will have given the students a taste of success, which is so important . . . . Success is important for everyone. So, through Drama, English becomes a living experience of communication.

To this we can add the findings of Susan L. Stern's informal study of a group of ESL students at the University of California at Los Angeles in 1977. These students were drawn from classes where the teachers had used a variety of drama activities as part of their teaching. The study returned the positive conclusion that drama encourages the operation of certain psychological factors in the participant which improve communication: heightened self-esteem, motivation, and spontaneity, increased capacity for empathy, and lowered sensitivity to rejection.

To sum up: we can list the potential benefits of drama in language teaching as follows:
- the acquisition of meaningful, fluent interaction in the target language;
- the assimilation of a whole range of pronunciation and prosodic features in a fully contextualized and interactional manner;
- the fully contextualized acquisition of new vocabulary and structure;
- an improved sense of confidence in the student in his or her ability to learn the target language.

The role of the teacher

If drama can really enrich the language class in all these ways, why are so many teachers reluctant to use it? Many still think of drama as 'theatricals', because this is their only experience of it. Often the fault lies not with the individual teacher, but with the training that he or she has received: a training that presents education as the one-way transmission of knowledge from the teacher to the student, rather than the creation of a learning situation in which the student is also the teacher.

Since the use of drama involves the formation of relationships and the breaking down of barriers between teacher and student, less confident teachers are understandably reluctant to use it. But, as Dorothy Heathcote (1972) points out:

> . . . we need to train our teachers to structure for a learning situation to happen rather than a sharing of information in a 'final' way to take place. We have to train them to with hold their expertise, to give their students opportunities for struggling with problems, before they come to the teacher's knowledge, and to reach an answer because of the work they do rather than the listening they have done. This will not lower standards, nor will it deny that which others have struggled painfully to achieve, nor will it 'waste' more time. What it will do is keep knowing at first hand alive, and thus encourage the desire for knowledge from those who went before.

The basic principle that Heathcote expounds here is that learners should be permitted to take responsibility for their own learning in such a way that the teacher can take a less dominant role in the classroom without losing the respect of the class or losing control.

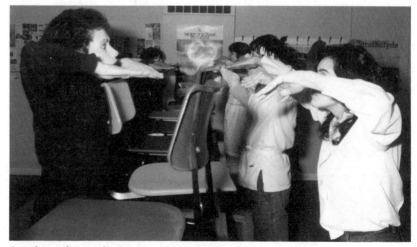

Breaking down the barriers between teacher and student

In the language-teaching situation, whenever the technique of drama is used, learners will constantly be confronted with the demands to take responsibility, to use their imaginations, to offer alternatives, to come up with solutions, and even to do some research (consulting dictionaries, interviewing others, and so on). And teachers should be ready to face and permit these 'challenges' to their authority. At the same time, this does not mean that such a lesson becomes chaotic and unstructured, which seems to be a predominant but baseless fear among some teachers.

On the contrary, the drama lesson should always be carefully planned and strictly timed and controlled. At the core of this planning is the decision on the aim of the lesson. Are we trying to teach a new structure? Reinforce previously taught language? Or trying to stimulate discussion? Whatever the aim, all the efforts of the teacher should be concentrated on it. Pacing and timing are all-important too, which is why each lesson in this book is accompanied by notes on these aspects.

What demands does drama make of the individual teacher?

Drama demands enthusiasm – not only for the lesson, but also for the students. And this in turn depends on the formation of a relationship of mutual trust in which neither teacher nor student feels 'at risk', but they willingly change roles and status to achieve the aims of the lesson.

Drama requires meticulous planning and structuring, and the ability to create a learning situation which will ensure a constant supply of stimuli to the students, which will keep them active and alert. And it depends on a willingness to take risks, assume roles, be seen as a 'real' person and to challenge the class constantly by assuming what Heathcote calls a variety of 'teaching registers', ranging from 'I-haven't-a-clue' to 'devil's advocate'.

We can sum it up in a nutshell: the desire to bring real life and truth into the classroom. It takes courage and practice to achieve this. Heathcote hopes for:

> a race of teachers who are unafraid to make relationships with classes, who are unafraid to admit they do not know, who never stop seeking to learn more about the dynamics of teaching; who bring all of themselves to school and work to suit the needs of their classes at any time so that learning is kept meaningful, who like to get on with the people they teach because they are unafraid of the dull, the aggressive, the unacademic, the 'naughty'; who are able to admit that they are tired today, so that their classes can take some responsibility.   (1972)

The role of the student

The typical student of English as a Foreign Language comes to the class with a 'shopping-list' of expectations. He or she wants to be able to read and write effectively in the language; to understand what English-speaking people are saying; and to be able to converse fluently and confidently in the language.

At the more advanced levels, there are students who require English for Academic and Specialist Purposes. They need English in order to write theses, to listen to lectures and take notes on them, and to participate in seminars.

In terms of expectations, we can say that all students are similar. But in terms of background and approaches to learning, they differ widely. The ideal language learner approaches the learning situation with an open mind, prepared to contribute widely and enthusiastically to the teaching programme, and to work independently of the teacher. The worst language learners (fortunately a rapidly decreasing minority) are totally dependent on the teacher, unwilling to participate in anything that is not obviously important to their own learning, and hostile to methods that conflict with the ones they are used to. These are the learners who are always asking for more grammar and more explicit rules. Their progress is painfully slow, and they blame their lack of success either on the course structure or on the teacher. Ironically, these are also the learners who will pick up most of their English in pubs and discos, unaware that they are using techniques that they would reject if they were introduced in class.

Between these two groups we have a number of variations. There are the students who will not say anything in the first few weeks until they have built up what they consider to be a reasonable repertoire in their minds (Japanese students, in particular, come to mind here). There are the students who, because of their cultural orientation, will find the teacher's frequent change of role and status degrading and distressing. And there are the students who will go along with all the activities in the class, particularly dramatic ones, but who will deny that they have taught them anything. We are reminded here of what Gavin Bolton (1984) says in this regard:

> Here then in drama we have a *unique pedagogic situation*, where a teacher sees himself as teaching but the participant does not see himself as learning.

We need to look at the ways in which we can introduce our students to drama without appearing either frivolous, aimless, or unstructured. In the first chapter of this book, we will set out ways in which this can be achieved. Dorothy Heathcote uses the phrase 'an edging in'.

Ultimately, what is required of the learner is an initial act of submission – an unspoken contract between the learner, the teacher, and the rest of the class in order to achieve the aims of the lesson. Only then can the student be said to be in a state of readiness for learning. Much will depend on the teacher's skilful handling of the class, and especially on the relationships built up between teacher and students in the crucial first week of a course.

The future

Drama in the teaching of languages requires further research, particularly in the areas of Languages for Special Purposes, and Academic and Professional Purposes. There is also a need for more rigorous research on the psycholinguistic benefits of using drama in language teaching, and we need more tangible evidence of the benefits derived from project work – can the improved performance of the student volunteer actually be measured and compared with that of the other non-project students?

It is to be hoped that coursebook writers, particularly in the field of English for Special Purposes, will incorporate more drama techniques in these books, so that the task and preparation of the teacher will be much simplified. We also need to examine more closely how drama techniques can be applied in the teaching of skills like reading, writing, and listening. So, the field is still wide open for future research and materials production.

Let me conclude with the words of renowned drama teacher, Keith Johnstone:

> As I grew up, everything started getting grey and dull. I could still remember the amazing intensity of the world I'd lived in as a child, but I thought the dulling of perception was an inevitable consequence of age – just as the lens of the eye is bound gradually to dim. I didn't understand that clarity is in the mind. I've since found tricks that can make the world blaze up again in about fifteen seconds, and the effect lasts for hours.   (1981)

For language teachers, the 'tricks that can make the world blaze up' are neither inaccessible nor impossible to use. We can find them in the basic human need to play and to create.

References and recommended reading

Bolton, Gavin. 1984. *Drama as Education: An Argument for Placing Drama at the Centre of the Curriculum*. London: Longman.

Dunlop, Frank. 1977. 'Human nature, learning, and ideology.' *The British Journal of Educational Studies* XXXV/3.

Hartley, B. and **P. Viney.** 1978–1985. *Streamline English (Departures, Connections, Destinations, Directions)*. Oxford: Oxford University Press.

Heathcote, Dorothy. 1982. 'Training needs for the future' in J. Hodgson and M. Banham (eds.): *Education I: The Annual Survey* (Pitman 1972). Reprinted in E. Johnson and C. O'Neill (eds.): *Dorothy Heathcote: Collected Writings on Education and Drama* (Hutchinson 1984).

Johnstone, Keith. 1981. *IMPRO – Improvisation and the Theatre.* London: Methuen.

Krashen, S.D. 1982. *Principles and Practice in Second Language Acquisition.* Oxford: Pergamon.

Maley, Alan and **Alan Duff.** 1982. *Drama Techniques in Language Learning.* Cambridge: Cambridge University Press.

Stern, Susan. 1980. 'Drama in second language learning from a psycholinguistic perspective.' *Language Learning* 30/1.

Via, Richard. 1972. 'English through drama.' *English Teaching Forum,* July–August 1972.

Wagner, Betty Jane. 1979. *Dorothy Heathcote: Drama as a Learning Medium.* London: Hutchinson.

Way, Brian. 1967. *Development Through Drama.* London: Longman.

Section One

Drama in the ELT classroom

1 'Edging in'

Introduction

What is it that we encounter as we enter a new class for the first time? It could be a roomful of complete strangers, or an already established group who have been together for some time, in which you, the English teacher, are the only stranger. If they are young children, you are in the happy position of dealing with natural actors and clowns, who like nothing better than a game. If they are adolescents, you will have to cope with the inevitable tensions they suffer because of their developing sexuality and physical changes. They will be terrified of being made to appear foolish in front of their peers. If they are adults, and have passed through a rigid, authoritarian system, they will tend to associate education and learning with 'being serious' and working hard. Languages, they will assume, can be learnt just like any other subject – a collection of facts that you stuff inside your brain and which somehow – hey presto! – comes out in an acceptable form.

Whatever the various groups and permutations within them, each student in a group is an individual with needs and longings often unexpressed. Yet within each, there is the spark of creativity. Carefully tended, this spark can be coaxed into a flame – the flame of communication. If you want to use drama as a teaching technique, you may need to encourage this spark by fanning the group until the flame catches. And then the process of learning through drama can actually start.

But it is a gradual process – if you arouse their hostility, if you demand entry to the students' creative selves without first unlocking the door, you might as well not use it. You will have to accept the fact that if a group doesn't want to be taught through drama, it should not be forced on them. Gradual and careful introduction and demonstrable success, enjoyment, and involvement is the way to convince the students of the value of learning through drama.

You are the key: the teacher as director-initiator

If you are planning to use drama techniques for the first time, allow yourself (and your students) a gradual induction period. By using techniques you feel at ease with, you will grow in confidence until you can attempt any type of dramatic activity. You will find a gradual release of more and more creative power within yourself, provided you allow it to happen naturally and spontaneously, and don't force it.

Students are very quick to pick up and expose any feelings of discomfort or uneasiness in a teacher. They may think, 'Well, if she is not comfortable with what she's doing with us, why should we accept it passively?'

It's the old confidence trick: stride in confidently, *believe* that it will work, and you can virtually sweep any class along. You may wish to start with a few games as 'ice-breakers' at the beginning of lessons, or as 'fillers' at the end. Some groups will happily accept these and look forward to more, while others will need to be told exactly why they are doing them. Then you may wish to turn your attention to the coursebook or grammar book. Carefully select those units that can readily be dramatized, and try out some of the techniques suggested in Chapter 3. You'll find that these units will definitely remain in their minds!

Classes in spoken communication skills lend themselves most readily to the addition of drama. With most classes, though, it is vital that some time is left for feedback at the end of such lessons. For this reason you should relinquish the centre-stage role after the activities have started and circulate – noting, prodding, helping, yet remaining on the fringes, having ready a set of comments on each student's language production. Recording or making a video of such activities are a great help, provided that such facilities exist and can be used easily by you or your students.

Remember at all times to be open to the needs of your students. Your body should reflect this 'openness' – a relaxed posture, an ease in being physically close to them, a warm, encouraging smile. But be firm at the same time – drama is not chaos, but order, meaningful order. As director-initiator you should always focus clearly on your aim and refuse to be side-tracked by other ideas that might defeat the aims of the lesson. But bear in mind those ideas that students put forward, even the ones you reject during a particular lesson, and use them at a later date. For those ideas may spring from actual needs within the student, needs which can and should be harnessed to the teaching process.

But to get back to the teacher: many of us are still blocked from experimenting with drama by the 'cult of personality'. Many times teachers and teacher trainees have exclaimed to me, 'It's all right for *you* to use drama, you've got the right personality for it!' Teaching skills are not related to personality only. Beneath individual style and personality can be a whole range of tools, devices, or strategies that authentic teachers can develop for themselves. It is this, plus constant attention to detail, that shapes the course of their teaching.

The right conditions for drama

In considering how to create the right conditions and the best atmosphere for drama, we encounter a paradox, for if we agree that drama pervades all aspects of life, then it is present even in the 'wrong' conditions and atmosphere. Perhaps it would be better to talk about the 'essential elements' which are required for a lesson using drama techniques to succeed. Seven of these elements are considered below.

Relationships

Students should be happy to work in groups or pairs, and all elements of strain should be removed. Help them to get to know, respect, and trust each other with a variety of 'getting to know you' techniques (see Chapter 2) and by the friendly atmosphere you create with your very first smile and lesson – your example is crucial, and should be a lead that they are willing to follow. Encourage positive comments as well as healthy criticism of each other's work. You can also encourage students to get to know each other better in social activities outside the classroom.

Physical environment

It should be easy to create space for physical activity in the classroom. This is the very first condition, as the students will often be required to get up and move around the room. At the same time, you do not want a bare, featureless room lacking in stimuli, in which the learners will be expected to be creative in a vacuum. A traditional classroom, with pictures, blackboard, reference books, and other audio-visual stimuli is still the best, as a bare room only creates inhibitions and stifles the imagination.

From the start, you should dispense with the traditional arrangement of desks with the teacher seated at the front of the room. There are at least five ways in which the classroom can be rearranged for drama activities. You may also want to experiment with lighting. Darkening the room and using a single light source, for example, the light from an overhead projector, can help to create atmosphere and sharpen the other senses.

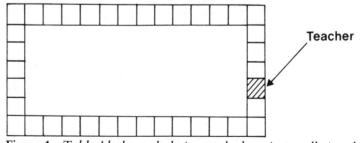

Figure 1: *Tables/desks and chairs stacked against walls (ready for use) with a large space in the centre. Suitable for games, mimes, and dramatized playreadings.*

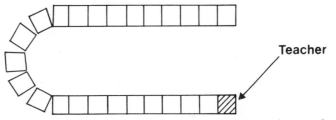

Figure 2: *Horseshoe/semi-circular arrangement (chairs only). Suitable for discussions followed by/following actions, pair and group work, plenary discussions, individual performances, and certain role plays.*

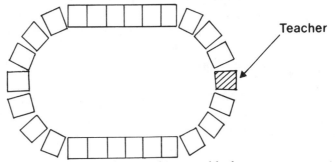

Figure 3: *Full circle (chairs only). Suitable for many games, simulations, and role play. Also good for seminar presentations.*

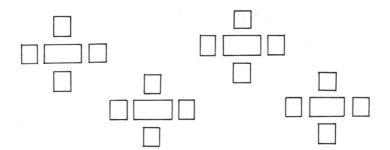

Figure 4: *'Grouped seating'—for simulations and other group activities. (Teacher circulates from group to group.)*

Figure 5: *The horseshoe arrangement again, but this time using desks. Suitable for most activities that also require reading and writing.*

Warm-ups

Depending on the type of lesson you are teaching, you may wish to prepare the group for it in a variety of ways. Apart from the introductory explanation or demonstration, some lessons, especially spoken communication skills or pronunciation lessons, benefit from such drama warm-ups as games, songs, or chants that are related to the main activity.

A background role for the teacher

From being the main source of knowledge in the classroom, you should gradually relinquish the centre-stage role, and become a *referent* rather than a guide. Students need to be made aware of their ability to learn from each other as well as to learn independently, and should be led into situations where they first exhaust all sources of knowledge themselves (reference books, dictionaries, encyclopedias) before asking you for help.

Goal orientation

Students should be aware that they are working towards a goal within a given time limit. This will sharpen their concentration, and help them to organize the group activities faster. And at the end of the lesson, they should have the satisfaction of having achieved that goal. So always ensure that they understand the aim of the lesson or activity.

Student leadership

Having group leaders will encourage in the students the sense of taking responsibility for their own learning. Boisterous, unresponsive, or plain lazy students should be given this responsibility.

Using the most co-operative students

Less inhibited and more confident students can be a great help in getting the others to co-operate. They can be used to demonstrate activities and to help with group work. Make sure that each group contains at least one of these students, as his or her presence will keep the group activity alive. Also team them up with more inhibited students for pair work. Remember to thank them (discreetly) for their assistance.

These seven elements are the key points in creating the right conditions and atmosphere for drama, and they have been listed in order of importance. Thus good relationships within the class, and the physical environment, are the most important ones.

The need for careful planning and timing

The success of any drama lesson depends partly on careful
planning, timing, and pacing. You need to decide how much time
you want to spend on each stage of the lesson. Figure 6 sets out the
essential components of a typical lesson using drama techniques; it
demonstrates the richness of such a lesson, and emphasizes the
need for careful timing.

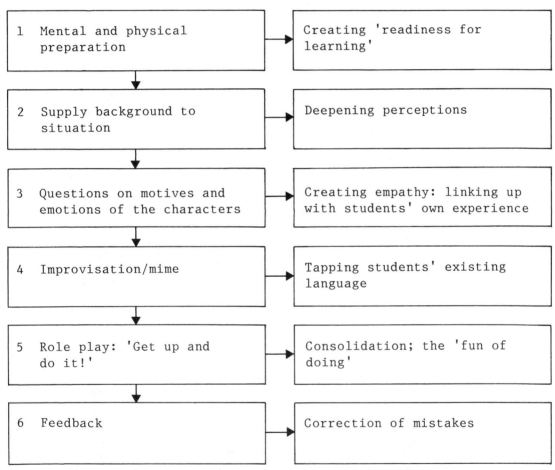

Figure 6: *The essential components of a lesson using drama techniques.*

Most, if not all, of these components are present in a drama lesson.
'Mental and physical preparation' here means the warm-up
activities, such as introductory games, which precede the lesson.
This could take up the first five or ten minutes of a lesson. 'Supply
background' means giving the lesson/dialogue/story a particular
context, thereby humanizing the situation, and giving it greater
substance and credibility. Again, this need not take up more than
five minutes. 'Questions on feelings and emotions' refers to the

questions that the teacher can ask to invite sympathy and empathy with the characters in the lesson, for example 'How does s/he feel at that moment? How would *you* feel in a similar situation?' Apart from such direct questions, an indirect approach is also effective, for example: 'Do you think s/he means what s/he says?' 'Is he really angry because of the trick played on him?' (which might elicit the response, 'No, he's just pretending'). This can take up to ten minutes.

The fourth and fifth components come into operation at the end of the lesson, when the students can be asked either to prepare similar situations and practise these new dialogues (role play), or to create new dialogues to extend the original one (improvisation), or to provide the language for a situation mimed by others. However, improvisation and mime can also occur at the beginning, or at other stages of the lesson.

The last fifteen minutes or so should be devoted to feedback. There are a number of ways in which this can be done. If you have been recording or filming the students, you can replay the video or cassette-recording and point out errors. If you have been making notes on errors during the activity, you can now discuss these errors with the whole class. Alternatively, there is the 'Hot Cards' system, where the teacher notes errors and their corrections on individual cards and then passes these on to the students concerned while the activity is still going on. Or you may prefer to listen to group work or pair work while moving around the class, and point out mistakes quietly to individual students without interrupting the flow of the activity. To allow for all these different aspects of the lesson, timing is a very important consideration.

Pacing, on the other hand, is far more difficult to plan, and will depend on the students' initial response to the materials. It is often quite surprising how students will get bogged down in minor details, and will refuse to be budged until they have sorted out that particular issue. In such a case, you could always promise a separate lesson on it, and focus them once more on the actual aim of the lesson. On the whole a brisk pace is recommended, aimed at the more competent students; or, if time permits, you could follow the lead of the class. At times their own experience of the unfolding drama will dictate how fast the lesson can move. Students can feel cheated if you try to hurry them through deeply-felt experience.

A common complaint of EFL teachers, particularly in European schools, is that lesson periods are often too short – 55 minutes, generally. This can place great constraints on teachers who wish to use drama, especially when they have a set syllabus to work through. Ideally, a drama lesson should last between one and a half and two hours, to permit the inclusion of the components outlined above. However, shorter lessons, if properly planned, can easily incorporate drama techniques.

How to evaluate a lesson incorporating drama techniques

We can measure the success of a drama lesson by asking a number of questions related to the two major objectives of using drama in language teaching:

1 overcoming resistance to the foreign language;
2 creating a need for speaking.

The notion of students 'resisting' the foreign language is not a new one, but one which still excites a good deal of controversy and argument. There is, I believe, a degree of resistance in every learner, varying in strength from person to person, and dependent on the learner's positive or negative attitude towards the language to be learnt, and the culture or nation from which it emanates. The learner's pride in his or her own language and culture will also influence the degree of resistance to the foreign language. Drama can be a very good ambassador for the new language.

Secondly, drama helps to create a need to speak by putting learners in situations where they feel compelled to speak. It could simply be a response to others during role play sessions, or becoming caught up in a situation that demands a solution, or by taking responsibility for a group activity as group leader.

The points set out in Table 1 need to be borne in mind when considering the merits of a drama lesson.

Criteria	
Objective 1: Overcoming resistance to the target language	**Objective 2**: Creating a need for speaking
a. Is the experience enjoyable? **b.** Are the targets realistic? **c.** Is there a creative 'slowing down' of experience? **d.** Can the lesson be linked to the students' own experience? **e.** Are the students in a state of readiness to learn?	**a.** Are there situations/problems that demand solution? **b.** Is responsibility placed on the learner? **c.** Would the lesson involve all the students, including the shyer or weaker ones?

Table 1

Let us examine what these questions mean, taking each objective in turn.

1 Overcoming resistance to the target language

a. *Is the experience enjoyable?* We have seen in the Introduction that the most basic reward of drama is that it is enjoyable. If we neglect this aspect, we put the entire drama lesson at risk by blocking the spontaneity and involvement that enjoyment brings to the lesson.

b. *Are the targets realistic?* This involves factors like the level of difficulty, the amount of work the teacher hopes to get through, and the accessibility of the situation for the learners. Naturally this ties in with factors like planning, pacing, and timing, as well as the readiness of the learners for that particular lesson.

c. *Is there a creative 'slowing down' of experience?* By this I mean a conscious attempt by the teacher to slow down the experience of the lesson to simulate the actual pace of real-life experience. This will incorporate factors like working out a suitable context for the situation, creating empathy with the characters involved, and acting out the story or dialogue. In other words, allowing the students to investigate the underlying reality of the situation instead of simply giving them the bare bones of the surface reality.

d. *Can the lesson be linked to the students' own experience?* This question is an attempt to link the activity to the real-life experiences of the students. Identification with any given situation is likely to increase their interest and involvement in it. This is, however, not a point worth overstressing, as experiences of life differ greatly. But wherever such identification is possible, it should be brought into play.

e. *Are the students in a state of readiness for learning?* In other words, have they been adequately prepared physically and psychologically for the activity?

2   Creating a need for speaking

The three questions related to this objective all carry with them the element of urgency. The learner should find it practically impossible to resist speaking, and drama creates this need by putting the emphasis on taking action to resolve a given situation or problem. As the teacher's role is peripheral rather than central, more responsibility is placed on the learners to work things out for themselves. Even shyer or weaker learners can become more involved in the activities by functioning as part of a group in which their contribution is just as important as that of the more extrovert learners. Many drama activities are specifically aimed at these weaker learners, to help them gain confidence in a non-threatening environment. In a sense, drama permits the subtle use of peer or community pressure on the individual in the classroom.

If the essential components of a lesson using drama techniques are present in your lesson, if you can answer 'yes' to most of the evaluation questions, then you are well on the way to applying drama techniques successfully in your own teaching.

2 Drama games

> Civilizations at their most complete moments always brought out
> in man his instinct to play and made it more inventive.
>
> (C.G. Jung)

In this chapter, we shall try to answer the questions *What are drama games?* and *Where can the language teacher apply them?* Then we will present a number of games which fit the definition and have been tried out successfully in EFL classes.

What are drama games?

All games have rules. A well-played game is the living embodiment of those rules, but a game filled with infringements of the rules, although it may contain the element of fun, is no longer a true game. In language teaching, too, games cannot be played successfully unless the rules have been clearly stated and understood by the learners. Therefore, games follow on a session of formal teaching, or form a living part of such sessions, in order, as Clive Barker says, 'to make the processes involved easier to understand' (Barker 1977).

Many 'structure games' have been devised to revise and reinforce particular areas of grammar, and these are, on the whole, fairly successful and popular with learners. However, once the required structure has been grasped, such games soon run out of steam and become repetitive. Is it possible to invent games that remain fresh and memorable?

At this point we need to state what we mean by 'drama games'.

A drama game involves action: Such games are rarely static. They call for movement and action around the whole classroom. Learners are invited to walk around the room, investigate its physical features and each other, to communicate with as many people as possible, and even to touch each other, however fleetingly.

A drama game exercises the imagination: The learners are called upon to 'see beyond' the teacher's presentation, to invent new situations or enliven existing ones with their own ideas, and to permit the dreams of their minds to flower into speech.

A drama game involves both 'learning' and 'acquisition': Unlike structure games, where the teacher wants the learner to reproduce the taught structure in a game-like context, a drama game generally practises far more language than just the core structure. It will always lead to some form of discussion among the participants, however inaccurately expressed that discussion may be.

A drama game permits the expression of emotion, linguistically and paralinguistically: As the learners have to empathize with the situations or persons they are asked to represent, they are given the freedom to express a whole range of emotions, not only in speech, but also through facial expressions and gestures.

These four elements distinguish drama games from other language games, and they give such games far wider scope and appeal than normal 'structure games'.

Where can drama games be used?

Basically, there are three major stages in a lesson at which games can be used most effectively. It must be understood, however, that the games referred to here are all short games, lasting from ten to fifteen minutes, and only a few can be extended to a full role play or improvisation.

Firstly there are 'icebreaker games' – games played at the beginning of a lesson as warm-ups or introductory activities. Such games tend to relax the learners, make them feel at ease with each other, and willing to work together. They also serve to introduce the main topic of the lesson. Often it is useful to combine two games at the beginning, one which simply breaks the ice, and one which leads in to the actual lesson itself. It is this stage that I referred to in Chapter 1 as the stage that creates 'readiness for learning'. And, of the three stages, this is the most important one.

Secondly, there are games used as part of a lesson, to revise or reinforce previously-taught material. Such games will generally be played before the 'exercise' or 'writing' stage in a lesson, and should help to clarify the taught material through direct experience. Games used at this stage are often the ones most readily accepted by the learners, because you do not need to justify them to the class – they are a natural progression of the lesson.

Thirdly, there are games which end a lesson (if time permits!). These can be used to 'unwind' the students after a hectic session of intensive learning, or simply as 'fillers'. Such games can help to revise the language taught during the lesson, and to 'fix' it in a relaxed and enjoyable manner. Sometimes, for a variety of reasons, a class can become unbearably dull, through no fault of yours. That is the time to stop whatever you are doing, and to enliven the class with some 'get up and do it' games.

Many of the games in this chapter, despite their grouping, can be used interchangeably. How you use them will depend on the class, and the materials to be presented. I generally find that I can fit in only one 'icebreaker' and one other game, either in the middle or at the end of the lesson. At other times, just one game will suffice.

Forty drama games: selection table

Starters

Game	Level	Ages	Preparation	Structures
Handshakes	All	All		
Cup ball	All	All	Yes	Numbers/alphabet
My name's X, etc.	All	All		Introductions
I'm X, and I'm from Z	Elem. +	All		Introductions/compounds
Interviews	Pre-int.+	All	Yes	Questions/reporting
Not me!	All	All		Accusations
Who am I?	Intermed. +	14+	Yes	Questions/descriptions
The four senses	Pre-int. +	All		General
Statues in the park	Pre-int. +	15+		General
Mirrors	All	All		General
The trust circle	All	All		(non-verbal)
Puppet on a string	All	All		General
Robot	Intermed. +	All		General/instructions
Moving pictures	Intermed. +	15+		General/instructions
Concentration	Elem. +	All		Numbers/names
Complaints	Pre-int. +	16+		Complaints
Alibi	Intermed. +	16+	Yes	Cause and effect
Whodunnit?	Pre-int. +	14+	Yes	Accusations/defence
Find your partner	Intermed. +	All	Yes	Questions/descriptions
Fear	Intermed. +	All		Emotions/physical reactions
What are we doing?	Pre-int. +	All		Verbs

In-betweens

Game	Level	Ages	Preparation	Structures
The preposition game	Pre-int. +	All	Yes	Prepositions
The article game	Intermed. +	16+	Yes	Articles
Taxi!	Pre-int. +	All	Yes	Conditionals
Feelings	Upper-int. +	15+	Yes	Emotions
Every picture tells a story	Intermed. +	All	Yes	General
Us and them	Intermed. +	All	Yes	Pronouns
Snake pit	Pre-int. +	All		3rd-person singular verbs
Tom's depressed	Pre-int. +	14+	Yes	General
The telephone call	Intermed. +	All	Yes	General
Watch the birdy!	All	All	Yes	General
Word association	Pre-int. +	All		General

Endgames

Game	Level	Ages	Preparation	Structures
Thank you	Pre-int. +	All		Adverbs
The music in me	Intermed. +	15+	Yes	General
Tribal chant	All	All		General
Quick-fire revision	All	All	Yes	
Any questions?	Pre-int. +	All		Questions
Ear to ear	All	All		
Simon says	Elem. +	All		Instructions
It's time to relax	Pre-int. +	All		Instructions/parts of the body

Starters/icebreakers

1 Handshakes

LEVEL	**All**
AGE	**All**
IN CLASS	Students circulate freely around the class, shaking hands with one another. On shaking hands, they simply say their names as loudly and clearly as possible, before moving on to the next person. This game is particularly appropriate for the very first session together.

2 Cup ball

LEVEL	**All**
AGE	**All**
STRUCTURES	**Numbers/alphabet**
PREPARATION	You will need a polystyrene cup for a 'ball'.
IN CLASS	Students stand in a circle, and hit the cup with upward strokes. The aim is to keep the 'ball' in the air as long as possible. With each stroke, they either count numbers together, or say the letters of the alphabet. The teacher should stress that everyone should count *together* whenever the 'ball' is hit and successfully kept in the air.

3 My name's X, and what about you?

LEVEL	**All**
AGE	**All**
STRUCTURES	**Introductions**
IN CLASS	Students sit in circles of not more than ten each. The first person starts off by introducing himself or herself: 'My name's X.' Turning to the left he or she asks the next person, 'And what about you?' That person responds, and passes the question on, until it comes back to the first speaker. Alternatively, the question can be asked of any person sitting in the circle, instead of consecutively.

4 I'm X, and I'm from Z

LEVEL   **Elementary upwards**

AGE   **All**

STRUCTURES   **Introductions/compounds**

IN CLASS   Students sit in a circle. Student **A** introduces himself, for example: 'I'm Ali, and I'm from Saudi Arabia'. Student **B** responds by saying, for example: 'You're Ali, and you're from Saudi Arabia. I'm Choi, and I'm from Korea.' Student **C** then says: 'You're Ali, and you're from Saudi Arabia. You're Choi, and you're from Korea. I'm Amanda, and I'm from Colombia.' The game continues until the last student has successfully listed everyone in the group. The game requires the students to *listen* attentively and to *speak* loudly and clearly.

5 Interviews

LEVEL   **Pre-intermediate upwards**

AGE   **All**

STRUCTURES   **Questions/reporting**

PREPARATION   Prepare three or four interview forms for each student, similar to the one shown here.

```
NAME:  .................................................

AGE:  ..............  JOB:  ...................

NATIONALITY:  ...............................

INTERESTS:  .................................

.............................................

BEST THING THAT EVER HAPPENED TO YOU:  .......

.............................................

WORST THING THAT EVER HAPPENED TO YOU:  ......

.............................................
```

Photocopiable © Oxford University Press

IN CLASS   The students circulate around the room, interviewing as many people as possible within the space of ten minutes. They then report back to the class on the people they have interviewed.

6 Not me!

LEVEL	**All**
AGE	**All**
STRUCTURES	**Accusations**

IN CLASS

The teacher starts the game by saying, 'It's John's turn to buy us all a drink/sing a song/cook us a meal.' The student named should respond, 'Not me! It's Peter's turn.' 'Peter' then responds, 'Not me! It's Anne's turn.' The game continues until everyone in the class has been named. Apart from familiarizing students with one another's names, this is a good way of practising the possessive case.

Note
An extension of this game is to draw up a list of jobs on the board first (to avoid running out of ideas) and to give each student a slip of paper with one of the jobs on it. S/he could then say, 'Not me! It's Anne's turn.' And Anne – if it was not her job – could respond genuinely with 'Not me! It's Peter's turn,' etc.

7 Who am I?

LEVEL	**Intermediate upwards**
AGE	**Fourteen upwards**
STRUCTURES	**Questions/descriptions**

PREPARATION

You will need slips of paper, one for each member of the class, each one bearing the name of a famous person.

IN CLASS

Pin or sellotape the name of a famous person on the back of each student. They then pair off and help each other to identify their characters. Student **A** asks questions such as *Am I alive or dead? Male or female? Young or old? Am I from Africa, Asia, Europe, or America? Am I a politician? A film star? A singer? If I am dead, how did I die? How old was I? What am I most famous for?* etc. Student **B** responds to the questions, but should try not to be too explicit.

If students find that they cannot help each other, they should move on to the next one, or to someone who can help them.

With a weak class, it might be helpful to put some of the above questions on the board before the game starts.

8 The four senses

LEVEL	**Pre-intermediate upwards**
AGE	**All**
STRUCTURES	**General**
IN CLASS	This is a game based on the senses of sight, hearing, taste, and feeling, concentrating on each one in turn.

Sight: The students are asked to study their right hands carefully, paying attention to details such as scars, callouses, length of fingers, distinctive lines, and the size of the hand. They are then asked to study a partner's hand with equal attention, and to discuss similarities and differences.

Hearing: The students are asked to shut their eyes, and listen carefully to all the sounds inside and outside the classroom. They then discuss what they have heard, and the teacher can list the sounds on the board.

Taste: With their eyes shut, the students concentrate on the taste of the last thing they ate or drank before coming to class. After a few minutes, they open their eyes and discuss this in pairs.

Feeling: This is played in pairs. Student **A** is blindfolded by Student **B**, who then gives him or her five different objects to identify through feeling alone. When he or she has successfully identified each object, Student **B** is blindfolded, and given five different objects to identify.

9 Statues in the park

LEVEL	**Pre-intermediate upwards**
AGE	**Fifteen and upwards**
STRUCTURES	**General**
IN CLASS	This game is played in pairs. Student **A** is the 'sculptor', Student **B** is the 'statue' being carved. The 'sculptor' shapes his or her subject into a famous statue, or at least one that is well-known to the students. Student **B** should be completely passive and obedient to the demands of the sculptor. When the statues are all ready, the sculptors walk around the class, admiring each other's work, and trying to identify the statues. The roles are then reversed, with the 'statues' becoming the 'sculptors', and the game proceeds as before.

A variation of this game is for the 'sculptor' to give only oral instructions to the 'statue'.

Some famous statues that could feature in this game: *the Statue of Liberty, Rodin's 'The Thinker', the Little Mermaid, Nelson's Column, Buddha, the Vénus de Milo, the Duke of Wellington, Napoleon, Joan of Arc, Atlas, and Michelangelo's 'David'.*

10 Mirrors

LEVEL	**All**
AGE	**All**
STRUCTURES	**General**
IN CLASS	This game is played in pairs. One person is just herself, performing activities such as cleaning her teeth, applying make-up, brushing her hair, dressing, etc. The other person is the 'mirror image', carefully copying everything done by the real person *as in a mirror*. For example, if Student **A** extends her *left* arm, Student **B** should extend her *right*. After a few minutes, the roles are reversed. This game can now lead to some verbal activities, rather like dubbing a film: **A** makes a sound, and **B** tries to copy it exactly; then **A** utters a short phrase, and **B** copies that; finally **A** utters a complete sentence, and **B** copies that, paying attention to correct intonation. They then switch roles, and continue as before.

11 The trust circle

LEVEL	**All**
AGE	**All**
STRUCTURES	**This is a non-verbal game.**
IN CLASS	Students stand in a circle, with one of them in the centre. This person allows himself to fall against the circle, while keeping his legs together and generally being as stiff as possible. Thus he is passed around the entire circle, after which it is someone else's turn. The game is called 'the trust circle' because the person in the centre has to trust in the rest of the circle to save him from falling over. Done correctly, it produces an effect similar to being rocked in a cradle.

Note: This game is best done after the first few weeks. It is not suitable for all groups.

12 Puppet on a string

LEVEL	All
AGE	All
STRUCTURES	General
IN CLASS	This game is played in pairs. Student **A** is the puppet, Student **B** the puppeteer. **A** cannot walk, move, or speak without **B**'s help. **B** has to support **A**, move **A**'s limbs, and be **A**'s voice. Together, they move around the room, interacting with the other puppets. After five minutes, the roles are reversed.

13 Robot

LEVEL	Intermediate upwards
AGE	All
STRUCTURES	General/instructions
IN CLASS	This game is similar to 'Puppet on a string'. This time **A** is a robot, and **B** her programmer. **A** has to do everything **B** tells her to do. The programmers can also direct their robots to do things to or with other robots. After five minutes, the roles are reversed.

14 Moving pictures

LEVEL	Intermediate upwards
AGE	Fifteen upwards
STRUCTURES	General/instructions
IN CLASS	Half the class is shown a picture of a group of people in a variety of attitudes. They arrange themselves into a copy of the picture (see the suggestions overleaf). Once this is done, the teacher informs the rest of the class that they are going to tell a story which will animate the picture. The teacher then starts the story, identifying the characters in the picture, and briefly sketching in some background details – where the people are, why they are there, what has happened to them so far. Then the class takes over, with each student speaking for about one minute and adding new details and action to the story. As the narration continues, the students forming the 'picture' respond in mime to the words of the narrators. The last student has to end the story in a satisfactory manner. The two groups then switch over, and a new story is told.

Photocopiable © Oxford University Press

15 Concentration

LEVEL	Elementary upwards
AGE	All
STRUCTURES	Numbers/names
IN CLASS	This game is played, seated, in a circle. The teacher is called 'Jack', and each student is given a number. The game is played to four beats, which are given by (a) slapping both hands on the thighs, then (b) clapping the hands together once, then (c) snapping the fingers of each hand in turn. So the beat is slap-clap-snap-snap. Everyone keeps their hands suspended above their laps, while the teacher chants CON-CEN-TRA-TION, then they slap their thighs, clap their hands, and on the first snap the teacher calls out 'Jack',

and on the second snap, any number of his choice. The student whose number has been called then calls out her own number and another number (or 'Jack'), while maintaining the beat. Anyone who breaks the beat becomes the new Jack, while the teacher becomes Number 1, and all the other numbers are changed. So with each new round, the students have to concentrate on their new numbers. The beat must not be broken or altered in any way.

16 Complaints

LEVEL	**Pre-intermediate upwards**
AGE	**Sixteen upwards**
STRUCTURES	**Complaints**
IN CLASS	The teacher asks the class about various situations in which they might wish to complain, and lists these on the board. Individual students then mime these situations, and the class have to guess which situation is being mimed.

The class can also be asked to suggest what the speaker could say in such a situation.

17 Alibi

LEVEL	**Intermediate upwards**
AGE	**Sixteen upwards**
STRUCTURES	**Cause and effect**
PREPARATION	Write cards for half the class accusing them of certain crimes, for example:

'You were seen running away from a bank after a robbery. The police will be here soon to take a statement.'

'You were seen climbing through your neighbour's window late last night.'

'Your uncle, who has left you all his money, died under mysterious circumstances. You were in his house on the night of the crime.'

Write alibi cards for the other half of the class, i.e. explanations that will provide the accused with a good excuse, for example:

'I had an urgent meeting and was late for it. I was unaware of the robbery. My colleagues at work will confirm that I was at the meeting.'

'I had gone to investigate a strange noise. My neighbour asked me to keep an eye on his house whenever he is out.'

'Yes, I was in the house, but I was speaking on the telephone to my cousin at the time of my uncle's death.'

IN CLASS   Distribute the cards. The accused students circulate in search of their alibis. When they meet up, they should discuss whether the alibi is strong enough. If they decide it isn't, they should create a better one.

18 Whodunnit?

LEVEL   Pre-intermediate upwards

AGE   Fourteen upwards

STRUCTURES   Accusations/defence

PREPARATION   Make a role card for each student, describing them as Lords and Ladies at the Court of King Cole. Use their own names, together with the title of 'Lord' or 'Lady'.

IN CLASS   When the role cards have been distributed and each participant has stated his or her title, the teacher solemnly announces, 'Somebody killed the king. I think it was Lord/Lady X.' The student accused defends himself, improvises an alibi, and promptly accuses someone else. Accusations fly around the room until they appear to centre on one person. The teacher then releases any negative tension by revealing the real identity of the killer – someone totally different.

19 Find your partner

LEVEL   Intermediate upwards

AGE   All

PREPARATION   Give each student a folder in which there is a picture.

IN CLASS   The students circulate, asking questions until each has found a 'partner' – a student with a picture of someone or something that can be matched with their picture. They should not say what they have in their folders, but through questions and descriptions they should lead each other to the right partnership.

20 Fear

LEVEL	**Intermediate upwards**
AGE	**All**
STRUCTURES	**Emotions/physical reactions**
IN CLASS	The teacher starts this game by asking the students how they feel and what happens to their bodies when they are afraid. These reactions are listed on the board; for example: hair standing on end, perspiring, sweaty palms, trembling, rapidly-beating heart, dry mouth, etc. Each student is then asked to list five everyday fears (excluding death by violence or accident). They then compare lists with a partner. A useful extension would be to introduce childhood fears, fears that have been overcome, and those still present. The partners can then offer each other advice on how to overcome these fears.

21 What are we doing?

LEVEL	**Pre-intermediate upwards**
AGE	**All**
STRUCTURES	**Verbs**
IN CLASS	This game is played in groups of three. Two people mime an action together, while the third tries to guess what they are doing.

Here are some suggestions which could be written on slips of paper and handed to the performing pair (each pair could be given two or three suggestions):

- A hairdresser cutting a difficult customer's hair.
- A bored doctor listening to a hypochondriacal patient.
- A waiter trying to flirt with an attractive girl eating in a restaurant.
- Two rich men trying to out-bid each other at an auction.
- Someone walking a very frisky dog.
- Two people quarrelling over which TV channel to watch.
- Two people moving a piano.
- Haggling over the price of an item in a market.
- Crossing a stream (with one person reaching out to help the other).
- Two people are attacked by a swarm of bees while enjoying a picnic; they get up and run away.

In-between games

22 The preposition game

LEVEL   **Pre-intermediate upwards**

AGE   **All**

STRUCTURES   **Prepositions**

PREPARATION   The first version of this game needs no preparation. For the second version, prepare ten cards, each bearing one of the following prepositions: *at, by, for, in, on, of, with, after, to, about*. Then prepare cards which each bear an incomplete sentence, such as:

'Are you afraid __ dogs?'

'I agree __ you.'

'I'm bad __ tennis.'

'We were sad to hear __ your illness.'

There should be at least three sentences for each preposition used in the game.

IN CLASS   This game can be played in two ways:

a. *In pairs:* one student calls out a preposition, and the other takes up or mimes the correct position, using either a desk or chair, to illustrate the preposition. See Figure 7.

Figure 7

b. *By the whole group:* pin the preposition cards described above on to ten students. Distribute the cards containing incomplete sentences to the rest of the students, who have two minutes to choose the correct preposition for their sentence. They should go and stand next to the appropriate student. (This game can also be used to teach phrasal verbs.)

23 The article game

LEVEL	**Intermediate upwards**
AGE	**Sixteen upwards**
STRUCTURES	**Articles**
PREPARATION	Choose four short poems, and write each one on a card. Then write each one again on another piece of card, but omitting all the definite and indefinite articles.
IN CLASS	This is a game that helps to sensitize students to the function of the article. Divide the class into four groups (if you have four poems). Half of each group is given a card containing a complete poem, and the other half gets the version with all the articles removed. They retire into opposite corners of the room, and practise saying the poems. The poems are then read aloud in groups, and they discuss the differences. Four poems that would work quite well are given below.

SAMPLE TEXTS

She's like the swallow that flies so high,
She's like the river that never runs dry,
She's like the sunshine on the lee shore.
I love my love and love is no more.
(Traditional)

There was a woman loved a man
as the man loved the sea.
Her thoughts of him were the same
as his thoughts of the sea.
They made an old sea chest for their belongings together.
('Sea Chest' – Carl Sandburg)

Sent as a present from Annam –
A red cockatoo.
Coloured like the peach-tree blossom,
Speaking with the speech of men.
And they did to it what is always done
To the learned and the eloquent.
They took a cage with stout bars
And shut it up inside.
('The Red Cockatoo' – Anonymous;
    translated from Chinese by Arthur Waley)

A lizard ran out on a rock and looked up, listening
no doubt to the sounding of the spheres.
And what a dandy fellow! the right toss
of a chin for you and swirl of a tail!

If men were as much men as lizards are lizards
they'd be worth looking at.

('Lizard' – D.H. Lawrence)

Note

An alternative version of this game is to issue all the students with
copies of the incomplete poems, and to let them decide, in pairs,
where articles should be inserted. They then read their completed
versions aloud, for comparison and criticism of the articles added.
Finally they are shown the complete poems.

24 Taxi!

LEVEL	**Pre-intermediate upwards**
AGE	**All**
STRUCTURES	**Conditionals**
PREPARATION	Make sets of 'if-cards' for the students who will play the part of taxi drivers. The cards dictate whom the taxis will stop for. For example: you may pick up a passenger

– if s/he is wearing red
– if s/he is waving with the *left* hand
– if s/he is taller than you are
– if you know the person's address
– if s/he is smiling.

IN CLASS	Appoint five students as taxi drivers, and give them each a set of 'if-cards' which tell them whom to stop for. They then start 'driving' around the class, while everyone else tries desperately to get a taxi. Once a taxi has picked up a passenger, he or she should be taken to the right destination before the taxi starts again (with a new 'if-card'). At the end, they can explain why they picked up only certain people.

25 Feelings

LEVEL	**Upper-intermediate**
AGE	**Fifteen upwards**
STRUCTURES	**Emotions**

| PREPARATION | Prepare cards – four for each student – with a feeling written on each card; for example, *love, hate, greed, envy, jealousy, grief, happiness, surprise, fear*, etc. |

| IN CLASS | This game is played in pairs. Each student gets four cards and has to mime the feelings written on the cards. The partners have to guess what the feelings are. |

Acknowledgement
I learned this game and the next one from my colleague Hélène Mulphin.

26 Every picture tells a story

| LEVEL | Intermediate upwards |

| AGE | All |

| STRUCTURES | General |

| PREPARATION | Make a collection of pictures of people doing various things. |

| IN CLASS | Divide the students into groups and give each group a picture. They have to devise a one-minute drama which will *end* with the group in the positions suggested by their picture. Each group presents its drama to the rest of the class, and when the teacher has shown the relevant picture to the class, they decide whether the group has successfully copied it. |

27 Us and them

| LEVEL | Intermediate upwards |

| AGE | All |

| STRUCTURES | Pronouns |

| PREPARATION | Prepare one card for each student. Each card contains half of a sentence which forms part of a group dialogue. |

| IN CLASS | This is a version of 'Split Exchanges', described by Maley and Duff (1982). Divide the class into two halves and give each student a card. They have to circulate in order to find that half of the sentence which completes their own. When this has been done, the two halves move to opposite sides of the room, and shout out the exchanges in the correct order, culminating in the battle cry, 'IT'S US OR THEM!'. |

This game is very useful for revising plural pronouns like *we, us, them,* and *they*. It also involves careful listening and clear projection when the exchanges are 'thrown around' the room. Short poems can also be used in this way (see Chapter 4).

SAMPLE TEXT

A
I wonder

the usual things.

Like – eating, drinking, and
– basketball!

be silly!

calling silly?
Don't get mad

They think

We shouldn't allow them

who's in charge around here!

or us!
It's us

B

what they're doing over there.
They're probably doing

Like what?

Basketball? Oh, now don't

Who are you

so quickly!

they're smarter than us.

to get away with it!
Let's show them

It's them

or them!

28 Snake pit

LEVEL   **Pre-intermediate upwards**

AGE   **All**

STRUCTURES   **Third-person singular verbs**

IN CLASS   Draw a chalk circle. One student stands in the circle, and relates the daily routine of someone well known to her. Whenever she omits the *-s* ending of third-person singular verbs, the class should hiss like snakes, while the teacher touches her with a 'snake', which means that she has been bitten. Three bites are fatal. The 'snake' could be a rule with a ribbon or rubber band attached to it, or a rubber toy snake. Each student chosen has two minutes in which to survive the snake pit.

Notes
Keep the atmosphere as relaxed as possible: the 'snake bites' must not be seen as a dreadful penalty for leaving off the *-s* ending, but

rather as a light-hearted reminder of the rule governing third-person singular present-tense verbs.

It is also possible to use this game for other structures, like articles (a 'bite' for each article omitted) and past-tense narratives (a 'bite' for each incorrect verb).

29 Tom's depressed

LEVEL — Pre-intermediate upwards

AGE — Fourteen upwards

STRUCTURES — General

IN CLASS — Choose one student to play the part of Tom. He is to sit in the centre of the class, looking as glum and depressed as possible (or you can put a 'sad' mask on him). In groups, the students decide on a list of things that would cheer him up, and arrange this list in order of merit. 'Tom' chooses the best selection, and the winning group then act out, in mime and speech, the first three things on their list. Alternatively, the students could simply re-arrange the following list in the best order: a flattering compliment; a bottle of champagne; a date with a lovely girl; a new car; dinner in the best restaurant in town; a new job; a better salary; a night at the disco; the latest LP by his favourite singer/group; a walk in the countryside.

An alternative version of this game is to ask the students to draw up a short list of situations/events/things/remarks which often depress them. They can then compare lists, and offer each other advice on how to overcome the depression.

30 The telephone call

LEVEL — Intermediate upwards

AGE — All

STRUCTURES — General

PREPARATION — Compose a telephone conversation between two people, and then write **A**'s words on one card, and **B**'s words on another. Each group of three students in the class will need an **A** card and a **B** card.

IN CLASS — Divide the class into groups of three. **A** has the words of one side of a telephone conversation, and **B** the other, while **C** observes. **B** should respond to **A**'s comments without any words, but with non-verbal sounds like *er, aha, mmm, uh, tsk!*, etc. **C**'s task is to guess which words these non-verbal sounds represent. She should write these down, and then compare them with the words of the original dialogue.

SAMPLE TEXT

A: Hallo. Is that you, Mary?
B: Mmm-mmm. (*yes*)
A: Well, I'm sorry to disturb you, but I wonder if you've finished with my typewriter?
B: Er . . . (*not quite*)
A: Can I have it back, please?
B: Uh-uh. (*no*)
A: Look – you've had it for three weeks now!
B: Mmm . . . (*that's true*)
A: I'm coming straight over to collect it, whether you've finished with it or not! (Slams down phone.)
B: Tsk, tsk! (*some people!*)

31 Watch the birdy!

LEVEL   **All**

AGE   **All**

STRUCTURES   **General**

PREPARATION   Find some pictures of groups of people in various poses, one picture for each group of five or six students.

IN CLASS   Divide the students into groups, and give them a picture each. Their task is to group themselves in the same positions as the people in the picture. The winners are those who most accurately reflect the picture they've been given. Alternatively, the groups could be asked to pretend that they are all members of the same family, posing for a family photograph. They need to decide whom they are going to represent, what the occasion is, who will stand closest to each parent, and why. They can explain their arrangement to the class afterwards.

32 Word association

LEVEL   **Pre-intermediate upwards**

AGE   **All**

STRUCTURES   **General**

IN CLASS

The teacher calls out a word, and the first student responds with a word that he or she associates with it. Then each one in turn responds to the word given by the previous student. After a few minutes, they 'pair off' and continue the game. But this time, the teacher interrupts them by shouting 'Why?'. Students then have to give reasons why they have chosen that word. Students should be encouraged to say the first thing that comes into their minds, i.e. not to block their true thoughts with more 'respectable' or 'conventional' ones. This could then lead to a creative writing session in groups or pairs; for example, the groups or pairs select ten of the words they have suggested, and these ten words must be worked into a short poem, containing one of the words in each line.

End-games

33 Thank you

LEVEL

Pre-intermediate upwards

AGE

All

STRUCTURES

Adverbs

IN CLASS

List a number of situations on the board, and ask the students how they would say 'Thank you' in each of these situations. The class can decide whether they agree with the way in which individual students respond. Here are some suggestions:

How would you say 'Thank you' if

- you have been given a present which you had once given to a friend of the person from whom you now receive it.
- a fellow passenger points out to you shortly before the train leaves that you are on the wrong train.
- the bus-driver waits for you to catch up with the bus.
- the postman brings you nothing but bills.
- an elderly person gave up his/her seat to you on the bus upon seeing that you felt ill.
- the doctor told you that you would probably live to a ripe old age.
- you got the job you really wanted.
- a stranger pays you an unexpected compliment.
- you win the booby prize in a competition.

34 The music in me

LEVEL	**Intermediate upwards**
AGE	**Fifteen upwards**
STRUCTURES	**General**
PREPARATION	Find some relaxing and romantic music to play to the class.
IN CLASS	This is a soothing end to a lesson. Students listen to the music with their eyes shut. Then students open their eyes, listen again, and jot down a number of words they associate with the music. They then explain the significance of these words to a partner.

35 Tribal chant

LEVEL	**All**
AGE	**All**
STRUCTURES	**General**
IN CLASS	Each student thinks of a particular sentence/phrase/word that he or she has learnt during the lesson. At a sign from the teacher they begin chanting these different expressions, first just one student, then another, then three, until everyone has joined in. The teacher could fire instructions from the side, for example: 'Chant happily/sadly/slowly/fast/angrily/tenderly', etc. Students find this good fun, and it tends to fix the words in their minds.

36 Quick-fire revision

LEVEL	**All**
AGE	**All**
PREPARATION	Have ready a set of twenty revision questions based on the lesson.
IN CLASS	Rapidly fire the questions at the students. All those who fail to answer within ten seconds are put in the centre space. They have to list three things they have learnt during the lesson before being allowed to return to their seats. Remember to keep the atmosphere fairly light-hearted.

37 Any questions?

LEVEL	Pre-intermediate upwards
AGE	All
STRUCTURES	Questions
IN CLASS	Pick a student to be the 'expert of the moment'. Seat him in front of the class, and allow each student to ask him one question relating either to the week's work or to the lesson. Keep track of his score, and allow him to compete with others, who can be the 'expert of the moment' on different days. Students score one point for each correct answer. Sample questions:

– What's the past tense of ____?
– What does ____ mean?
– How do you spell ____?
– What do you say when ____?

38 Ear to ear

LEVEL	All
AGE	All
IN CLASS	Students stand in a circle. Take any complex sentence from the lesson, and whisper it in the ear of Student **A**. The sentence is passed along the circle by whispering. The final student is then asked to say the sentence out loud. Usually this will differ greatly from the original sentence. The class should then work out where it went wrong, and chant the sentence out loud. Then they start the next round, moving in a different direction this time.

39 Simon says

LEVEL	Elementary upwards
AGE	All
STRUCTURES	Instructions
IN CLASS	The teacher or one of the best students acts as 'Simon'. The students stand in a square, facing 'Simon', who then gives them various instructions, for example, 'Simon says sit down'; 'Simon says touch the floor', etc. But 'Simon' also gives instructions

without the use of 'Simon says'. Any student who obeys these instructions falls out. The game continues until only one student remains, who is declared to be the winner.

Notes

As students can rapidly run out of instructions to give, it is advisable to write some on the board, for example:

- scratch your head
- pull your ear
- point your toe
- clap your hands
- close your eyes
- kick your leg
- roll your neck
- show your teeth, etc.

It might also help to introduce a few 'props', for example a stick, a bottle, a newspaper, etc. which can then become part of the instructions, e.g. 'pass the stick/read the newspaper/roll the bottle', etc.

40 It's time to relax

LEVEL	**Pre-intermediate upwards**
AGE	**All**
STRUCTURES	**Instructions/parts of the body**
IN CLASS	This can be done with the students either lying on the floor or sitting on chairs. Talk them through the various parts of their bodies, starting with their toes, and working up to their scalps: 'Tense your toes . . . and relax them. Now tense your calves . . . and relax them. Tighten your knees . . . and relax. That's right . . .', etc. When you reach the tops of their scalps, just let them lie or sit quietly for a while. Then, very slowly, let them get up. Throughout, your voice should be relaxed and neutral.

References and recommended reading

Barker, Clive. 1977. *Theatre Games*. London: Methuen.
Maley, Alan and **Alan Duff.** 1982. *Drama Techniques in Language Teaching*. Cambridge: Cambridge University Press.

3 Improving coursebook presentation through drama

Introduction

So many teachers, particularly those working in primary and secondary education, are stuck with a coursebook and have no room to move, nor any access to supplementary materials. Ways of supplementing and enlivening the coursebook are much needed if learning is to be made meaningful and enjoyable for both teacher and students. This chapter suggests ways in which this can be achieved through drama. It is addressed particularly to those teachers whose sole teaching aid is the coursebook.

There has been a significant improvement in EFL coursebooks over the past decade. Most of them employ drama techniques such as role plays, dialogues, games, and simulations, and so they should, in theory at least, lead to genuine communication between the learners. But too few guidelines are given to the teachers on how to exploit these techniques to their maximum potential, and rarely are students expected to try and see beyond the message of the printed page, or to use their imaginations to bring the situation to life. What generally happens is a 'read-through' of the dialogues, followed by comprehension questions and role plays in which students simply copy the words of the original dialogue. In other words, short-term learning takes place which does not truly extend the students' knowledge and use of the target language.

Thus the teacher, with the co-operation of the class, has to strive to make the coursebook come alive – to make the characters and their actions *stand up* from the printed page and become people with real-life feelings and needs. Drama can help the teacher to achieve this 'reality' in several ways. It can overcome students' resistance to learning the new language:

- by making the learning of the new language an enjoyable experience;
- by setting realistic targets for the students to aim for;
- by the creative 'slowing down' of real experience;
- by linking the language-learning experience with the students' own experience of life.

And drama can create in students a *need* to learn the language:

- by the use of 'creative tension' (situations requiring urgent solutions);
- by putting more responsibility on the learner, as opposed to the teacher.

Drama is like a condiment that can be used to spice up the coursebook. And, like most condiments, it is best used sparingly and with discretion – teachers should not expect it to work with all aspects of the coursebook. It is often enough to use it intensively in the first few weeks of a course, because students will tend to dramatize their coursebook dialogues and role plays without prompting from the teacher once this basic pattern of teaching has become familiar to them. After the intensive use of the first few weeks, only the occasional lesson that requires dramatization should be presented. So we should establish a basic pattern of dramatic teaching of the coursebook initially, and then allow the students to take over and do it themselves.

Extending coursebook materials

Two techniques are already used by many teachers in their coursebook presentation: warm-up games or related activities like songs or chants, and dramatized reading, in which students are encouraged to read with feeling and sometimes to add gestures and movements to paired or group reading of the coursebook dialogues. What else can we add to these basic techniques?

Mime

Many teachers use mime without even being aware of it. Where words fail (as in explaining new vocabulary), a quick mime helps to convey the meaning. Many of the games in Chapter 2 use mime, as do a large number of grammar games. For example, verbs and adverbs can be both taught and reinforced through mime (see *What are we doing?* in Chapter 2). Coursebook dialogues can also be presented in mime, with selected students doing the mime, while the rest of the class try to match the words of the dialogue to the actions. Even the weaker students can increase in confidence through the use of mime, as it can help them to gain an understanding of the lesson without having to use the words initially.

Improvisation

By the time the students have reached the pre-intermediate stage, they should have enough language to improvise possible continuations of dialogues, or to predict what might have preceded and led up to the dialogue. Through improvisation they can break free of the confines of the dialogue and create their own script, while still using the original context (see Sample Lesson 2 in this chapter). They can even be asked to suggest background details for the characters in the dialogues – their home life, status, attitudes and ambitions, past experiences, and so on.

Speculations on feelings and thoughts

By asking questions about the thoughts and feelings of the coursebook characters, we can help our students to empathize with these characters and to see beyond the printed page. But we should avoid direct questions like 'How do they feel?' (which simply lead to routine answers like 'They feel angry'), and try to lead them to speculation rather than explanation. For example, questions like 'Why does he slam the door?', 'Why does she stress the word *want*?', 'Why doesn't she thank them for the present?' are far more likely to stimulate imaginative answers and to 'stretch' the students linguistically.

Adding stage directions

This activity, which can be done in the mother tongue of the students, helps students to link paralinguistic features like gesture and facial expressions with the language itself. It also helps to sensitize them to the ways in which various feelings are expressed in the target language. Students enjoy thinking up ways in which the lines can be said, and then comparing their interpretation with the teacher's or that of the accompanying tape recording. (See Sample Lesson 1.)

Parallel role plays

The language of the original dialogue can be practised through a parallel dialogue that requires the same speech acts and vocabulary as the original one. Sample Lesson 2 has an example of such a parallel role play.

Lengthening and shortening the dialogue

Students can be asked to lengthen dialogues (for example by the insertion of adjectives, adverbs, embedded clauses, conversational gambits, etc.), or to shorten them (perhaps to the level of one-word utterances).

Three sample lessons

To illustrate the use of these techniques, here are three sample lessons taken from coursebooks in current use. Sample Lesson 1 is intended for use with elementary students, Sample Lesson 2 is for pre-intermediate students, and Sample Lesson 3 is for intermediate students of Business English. Suggestions for warm-ups or introductory activities have been included, together with notes on timing and pacing.

Sample lesson 1: 'Rick's late'

SOURCE	*Network 1* (by J. Eastwood, V. Kay, R. Mackin, and P. Strevens, published by Oxford University Press, 1980)
LEVEL	Elementary
TIMING	About 60 minutes
PACING	Fairly slow at first, to allow for complete integration of words, actions, and feelings.
WARM-UPS	1 'Late again' (a dialogue for rhythmic chanting, from *Jazz Chants* by Carolyn Graham, published by Oxford University Press, 1978) 2 'Not me!' (a game for practising the language of accusations; number 6 in Chapter 2 of this book)
PREPARATION	The main technique in this lesson is the addition of stage directions to the coursebook dialogue. The teacher should prepare, in advance, typed copies of the original dialogue (opposite), and should include directions (in the students' mother tongue) on movement, emotions expressed, gestures, and facial expressions. But if the teacher does not speak the language, or if the class is a multilingual one, the variation outlined at the end of this sample lesson should be used.
IN CLASS	1 Issue students with copies of the typed dialogue. They should not, at this stage, open their coursebooks. Students do silent reading of the text and stage directions. 2 Students listen to a recording of the dialogue while following it on their handouts. This helps them to understand how emotions are expressed in the target language – how the intonation, stress, and rhythm change according to the emotions expressed; a video recording would show them which gestures and facial expressions would accompany the spoken utterances. 3 Now instruct the students to open their coursebooks and to add the stage directions themselves. They then read the dialogue in pairs, and comment on each other's performances. 4 Now do the accompanying exercises in the coursebook.

SAMPLE TEXT

1 The original version

Robert Black: Rick!
Rick Strong: Hello. Am I late?
Robert: Yes, you are. *Why* are you late?
Rick: Oh. Well, I have no transport.
Robert: No transport? Why not?
Rick: Well, my girlfriend has my car. And I have no watch.
Robert: No watch? Why not?
Rick: Well, my girlfriend has my watch.
Robert: Rick, you're very late. Go to the studio!
Rick: Yes, Robert.
Robert: And buy a bicycle!
Rick: Yes, Robert.
Robert: And buy a new watch!
Rick: Yes, Robert.
Robert: And find a new girlfriend!
Rick: No, Robert.

2 The expanded version
Note that the stage directions have been written in English for
convenience, but they should of course be written in the learners'
mother tongue.

(*Rick comes hastily into the room. He nearly collides with his superior,
Robert Black. Robert is frowning, while Rick looks very embarrassed.*)
Robert Black: (*angrily*) Rick!
Rick Strong: (*flustered*) Hello. Am I late?
Robert: Yes, you are. *Why* are you late?
Rick: Oh. Well . . . I . . . I have no transport.
Robert: (*disbelieving*) No transport? Why not?
Rick: Well . . . my . . . girlfriend has my car. And (*holds out his
wrist*) I have no watch.
Robert: (*incredulous*) No watch? Why not?
Rick: (*sheepish*) Well, my girlfriend has my watch.
Robert: (*still angry, commanding*) Rick, you're very late. (*points*) Go
to the studio!
Rick: (*meekly*) Yes, Robert. (*starts to leave*)
Robert: (*less angry than before*) And buy a bicycle!
Rick: Yes, Robert.
Robert: (*beginning to smile*) And buy a new watch!
Rick: (*beginning to relax*) Yes, Robert.
Robert: (*laughs*) And find a new girlfriend!
Rick: (*emphatic*) No, Robert. (*laughs, and exits*)

VARIATION

If you do not speak the students' first language, or if you are dealing
with a multilingual class, write down all the stage directions on the
board. Now ask the students to consult their dictionaries, and to
write down the meanings of the stage directions in their mother
tongues. Then show them where to add these stage directions, and
proceed as above.

Sample lesson 2: 'Complaints'

SOURCE   *Encounters* (by J. Garton-Sprenger, P. Prowse, and T. Jupp, published by Heinemann, 1979)

LEVEL   **Pre-intermediate**

TIMING   **About 90 minutes**

PACING   **Quite brisk**

WARM-UPS   **'My feet hurt'** (from *Jazz Chants* by Carolyn Graham, published by Oxford University Press, 1978)

IN CLASS   This is a lesson employing a number of dramatic techniques from beginning to end.

1 Ask students to suggest various things we can complain about. List these on the board.

2 Choose a few students to come out and to mime any of the complaints situations of their choice. The class have to guess which situation is being mimed, and should supply the words of the student mimic.

3 Creating background: ask the class about David and Sarah's stay at the hotel. Did they complain about anything? Did they enjoy their stay?

4 Silent reading of the dialogue.

5 Listening to the dialogue on cassette.

6 Post-listening activity: speculation on the feelings of the speakers. List the feelings on the board. What would the students do if they were in a similar situation?

7 Practise the stress and intonation of the dialogue, for example, 'I *want* to see the manager'; 'I *do* apologize'.

8 Group readings of the dialogue, paying particular attention to correct stress and intonation.

9 The students answer the comprehension questions in pairs.

10 Ask students to suggest a continuation of the dialogue.

11 Now do the Practice session of this lesson (reprinted below). Issue students with a menu, take their orders, and give them the wrong bill. (These activities could be done by a competent student.) This will stimulate them to use the language presented in the practice session.

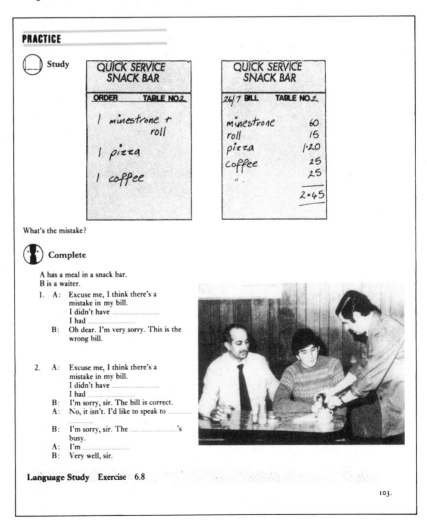

PRACTICE

⊖ **Study**

QUICK SERVICE SNACK BAR

ORDER   TABLE NO.2

1 minestrone + roll

1 pizza

1 coffee

QUICK SERVICE SNACK BAR

26/7 BILL   TABLE NO.2

minestrone   60
roll   15
pizza   1·20
coffee   25
" .   25
             ‾‾‾‾‾
             2·45

What's the mistake?

🙂 **Complete**

A has a meal in a snack bar.
B is a waiter.

1. A: Excuse me, I think there's a mistake in my bill.
       I didn't have ....
       I had ....
    B: Oh dear. I'm very sorry. This is the wrong bill.

2. A: Excuse me, I think there's a mistake in my bill.
       I didn't have ....
       I had ....
    B: I'm sorry, sir. The bill is correct.
    A: No, it isn't. I'd like to speak to ....
    B: I'm sorry, sir. The ....'s busy.
    A: I'm ....
    B: Very well, sir.

Language Study   Exercise 6.8

103.

Sample lesson 3: 'Recruitment and selection'

SOURCE   *Manage with English* (by P.L. Sandler and C.L. Stott, published by Oxford University Press, 1981)

LEVEL   Intermediate

TIMING   Stages 1–4: 30–45 minutes

PACING   Moderate

PREPARATION   Prepare a number of job advertisements, and put these on the class notice-board. Imaginary, fanciful ones will work particularly well, and by being humorous will have the advantage of relaxing the students while still eliciting the language needed. Examples are given below.

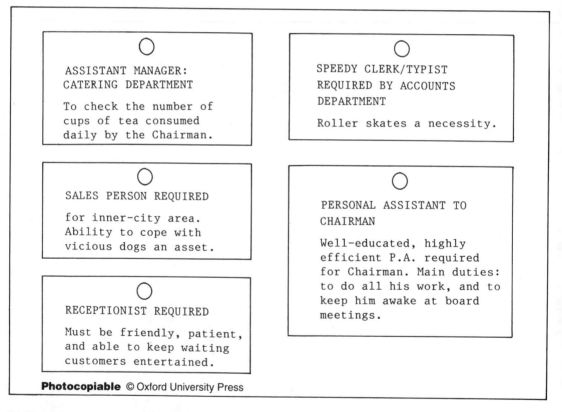

ASSISTANT MANAGER:
CATERING DEPARTMENT

To check the number of cups of tea consumed daily by the Chairman.

SPEEDY CLERK/TYPIST
REQUIRED BY ACCOUNTS
DEPARTMENT

Roller skates a necessity.

SALES PERSON REQUIRED

for inner-city area. Ability to cope with vicious dogs an asset.

PERSONAL ASSISTANT TO
CHAIRMAN

Well-educated, highly efficient P.A. required for Chairman. Main duties: to do all his work, and to keep him awake at board meetings.

RECEPTIONIST REQUIRED

Must be friendly, patient, and able to keep waiting customers entertained.

Photocopiable © Oxford University Press

IN CLASS   1 As students file into class for the lesson, let them read the job advertisements and ask them to choose which job they would like to apply for.

2 Students discuss which jobs they would prefer and why. This stage could be done in pairs, followed by a report-back session to the whole class.

3 Students each complete a brief *curriculum vitae* with information about themselves. You could either write an outline on the board, or prepare blank forms in advance. An example is given below.

```
NAME ...........................................................................

ADDRESS .......................................................................

AGE ........................      NATIONALITY ...............................

SEX ........................      MARITAL STATUS ...........................

EDUCATION .....................................................................

...............................................................................

QUALIFICATIONS ................................................................

...............................................................................

LANGUAGES .....................................................................

INTERESTS .....................................................................

POST APPLIED FOR ..............................................................
```

4 The students discuss in pairs which job would suit each of them best, on the basis of their *curricula vitae*. This should be followed by a brief plenary session with the whole class. (It will be a light-hearted activity, owing to the nature of the jobs advertised.)

5 Now introduce the reading passage from the coursebook, and do the follow-up activities.

Unit 1   Recruitment and Selection

Read the following passage.

When there is a vacancy in a company, it is the job of the Personnel Manager and his department to manage the recruitment of a new employee. One way an organization can find staff for job vacancies is to recruit in-company. Management can inform people of new appointments by means of the firm's notice board or news bulletin. Another possibility is to ask for recommendations from departmental managers and supervisors. If it is necessary to recruit outside the company, the personnel department may use commercial and government employment offices or consultants. It may prefer to put its own advertisement in a newspaper or magazine.

It is usual for an advertisement to give a short description of the job, conditions of work and salary, and to invite introductory letters from applicants. After studying these, management decides who receives an application form.

In order to assess the applications, managers can work from a personnel specification such as Rodger's Seven-Point Plan. They do not choose applicants who do not have a good profile. For this reason, it is important that the application form requests clear information about such things as the applicant's age, education, qualifications and work experience. It must also ask for references from other employers or people who know the applicant well. This information helps management to make a final decision on the number of applicants they can short-list for interview.

The staff who hold an interview together are called an interview 'panel'. It is important that they know what information they need to get from the applicants. This comes from a careful reading of job descriptions, personnel specifications, and applications. To help the panel in their selection, some companies use an interview assessment form. This is used by the panel during the interview when each applicant is checked under the same point on the form.

Many employers say that the success of a good business begins in the Personnel Manager's office.

4 Drama in the teaching of pronunciation

If there were some easy, quick method for making people flexible enough to change vocal habits quickly and radically, it would probably have been discovered long ago. The fact is that vocal flexibility is the result of experience, lots of practice, and attention to many small, but important, factors that many people are not aware of or do not care about. Posture is one. Breathing is another. Breathing and posture are related. If we have good posture, our breathing is easier. If our breathing is more under control, then so are our voices.

(Stephen Smith: *The Theatre Arts and the Teaching of Second Languages*)

Introduction

Language teachers can learn a great deal from the way in which actors prepare their voices for the stage. The techniques presented in this chapter can be said to be a reaction against the 'standard' methods of teaching pronunciation, which are basically listening to and repeating certain sounds, words, and phrases, which are often uncontextualized and therefore difficult to remember. The techniques to be described acknowledge that speech is more than simply repeating what you hear, and that the shape of the mouth, posture, the mechanics of breathing, and even facial expressions are part and parcel of correct pronunciation. Honikman's successful teaching of the correct 'mouth-set' for French with her students is a fine example of how we can help learners to become more aware of the technical equipment of correct pronunciation (see Honikman 1964).

In the appendix of Clifford Turner's most useful book, *Voice and Speech in the Theatre*, Malcolm Morrison outlines typical voice and speech routines for the actor. These include:

– relaxation and posture: exercises designed to release tension;
– breathing: learning to control and utilize breathing fully;
– tone: learning to use the whole resonator (mouth, nose, and pharynx) to produce sounds;
– pitch: exercises which practise the rise and fall of the voice;
– articulation: reciting tongue-twisters, chants, or bits of poetry to secure clear speech.

Let us examine each of these in turn, to see whether they are relevant to a language learner. Firstly, the twin issues of *relaxation* and *posture*. When we are tense, our bodies become stiff and rigid. We hunch our shoulders and breathe in a shallow way, our mouths become dry, and our voices tighten up as well. And on top of that, in a foreign-language class, we are then asked to read aloud, or to produce sounds, in a language totally foreign to our own. No matter how hard we try, it is impossible to utter the right sounds, for we can only utter what we 'hear'. We can neither 'see' nor 'feel' the sound. Our rigid bodies in turn affect the way we breathe, and without control over our breathing we cannot use our voices fully.

Relaxation exercise

Next, the question of *breathing*. 'The breath is seen to be the foundation upon which utterance is built', says Turner. In everyday life, breathing is a normal reflex, carried out unconsciously by everyone. Actors, however, consciously direct their breathing until new habits are formed that will ensure the best results in the voice. In the same way, learners of a foreign language need to direct their breathing consciously to produce the correct sounds in that language, until the habit of doing so has been fully acquired.

Tone comes next in the order of training of an actor. It is principally concerned with learning to use the resonator of the voice, which consists of the pharynx, the mouth, and the nose. It is a speaker's tone that helps us to recognize his voice over the telephone, even before he has identified himself. As Turner says:

> Various adjectives are brought into service to express the effect made on our senses by voices of different quality. We speak of the tone of voices as bright or dull, rich or thin, hard or soft, pleasing or raucous, irritating, maddening, and doubtless other epithets will occur to the reader!

The major aspect of tone which concerns the language learner is learning to use the mouth, with its movable tongue, lips, and jaws correctly, in order to assume the precise 'mouth-set' of the foreign language.

In language teaching, pitch is called *intonation*. No language-teaching programme is complete without it, but there are too few books and other materials available to the language teacher at present. Therefore teachers need to be shown ways of devising their own materials in order to incorporate pitch into their teaching. Actors learn to hum, chant, or sing in rising or falling pitch, as shown in Figure 8.

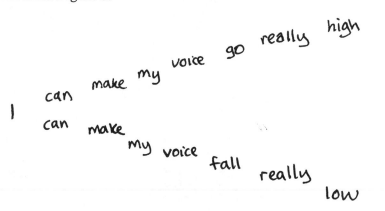

Figure 8

These exercises are often aided by piano accompaniment.

Finally, *articulation*. This is one area of an actor's training which has been incorporated to some extent in language teaching. These exercises are also called 'vocal warm-ups', and are designed to help learners to distinguish between related sounds by letting them chant tongue-twisters like 'She sells sea-shells on the sea-shore', minimal pairs like 'papapa/bababa/tatata/dadada/kakaka/gagaga', or snatches of poetry which include sounds that are particularly difficult for a particular group of learners. For example, this extract from Masefield's 'Reynard the Fox' might prove quite difficult for Oriental students:

> Like a rocket shot to a ship ashore
> The lean red bolt of his body tore
> Like a ripple of wind running swift on grass
> Like a shadow on wheat when a cloud blows past.

Students start off by chanting together, then in pairs, and eventually on their own, once they signal confidence and willingness to do so.

Does this mean that we can dispense with all the pronunciation books and cassettes that have been produced so far? Not at all. The learners will still need time for individual study, and teachers who are not native speakers will still need good models of 'standard' pronunciation. But by incorporating drama techniques into the teaching of pronunciation, we can stimulate in our students deeper awareness and understanding of what goes into the production of those sounds on the cassette, and this will make the process of individual pronunciation practice more meaningful and productive.

The teacher's role

As teacher, you need to be an active participant in all the activities outlined on the following pages. You will be the main model for all the sounds produced, and also for all the breathing exercises. A lively, brisk tempo needs to be maintained. Give short, crisp orders like *Repeat, Do this, Again, Say* ____, and so on, followed by your own actions and words. You will also need to 'conduct' some of the choral activities, using your arms and hands to indicate which section of the class should speak. Above all, you need to be entirely convincing in your presentation of these methods. Allow for the initial laughter, but insist that they need to concentrate carefully on each stage of the lesson in order to learn about the difficulties of pronunciation in the foreign language. If you are unsure about the methods, try them out first with a group of fellow teachers.

Teaching pronunciation and prosody to beginner and elementary students

The following exercises can be used either together as a set, or individually as part of other pronunciation or speaking lessons. In the first case, a typical lesson will include the following exercises:

– relaxation and posture;
– breathing, leading on to tone and pitch exercises;
– one or more of the following: copying mouth-set; projecting clearly; learning rhythm; group chanting/choral reading; stress and intonation;
– paired/group practice, with individual assistance from the teacher.

In the second case, you can either start or finish a lesson with one of these exercises, in addition to practice with model pronunciation cassettes either in class or in the language laboratory.

Relaxation and posture

Instruct the students to stand up straight, legs slightly apart, shoulders relaxed, and head upright (it would help if they focused on something at eye-level). Now instruct them to rotate their necks slowly, four times to the left, and four times to the right.

Next, instruct them to roll their shoulders backwards; first the left shoulder four times, then the right shoulder four times, finally both shoulders together eight times.

Now tell them to inhale and raise their arms to shoulder-height, then to exhale and raise them above their heads. Keeping both arms in that position, they should stretch up ten times with the right hand, and then ten times with the left. After that, they should inhale and lower their arms to shoulder-height, then exhale and lower their arms to their sides.

Finally, ask them to stand in a circle, and then to turn to the left. They should then reach out to the shoulders of the person standing in front of them, and very gently massage that person's shoulders and neck, while being massaged themselves.

You can give the instruction in the students' mother tongue, or in English, together with a practical demonstration of what you want them to do. Keep your voice gentle and even, and remember to do each exercise slowly and without straining any muscles. With more inhibited groups you may wish to omit the final group massage (although I have personally found it a most effective ice-breaker). In these cases, simply insist on the correct stance as outlined above. Explain why correct stance promotes good and clear pronunciation.

Breathing, incorporating some tone and pitch exercises

Now instruct the students to place their fingers on their ribs with the thumbs behind, pointing towards the spine, three or four inches above the waist just in front of the armpits. Tell them to breathe silently, and to feel the movement of their chests. Ideally, they should breathe laterally, i.e. *outwards* and not up. You could walk around and feel whether this is in fact the case. Continue this exercise for five minutes.

Next, relax their jaws by instructing them to breathe in through their noses, and, silently, release the breath through their mouths. They should inhale for three counts, hold it for three, and exhale for three. Do this for a further five minutes.

From the above exercise, go into the following tone exercises:

a. Inhale, and let out the breath on a long AAAAAAAAAH. /ɑ:/
b. Inhale, and let out the breath on a long OOOOOOOOOH. /u:/
c. Inhale, and let out the breath on a long EEEEEEEEEE. /i:/
d. Now do the same with MMMMMMMMMM and NNNNNNNNN.
e. Now practise combinations of the above, i.e. MMMMAAAA; MMMMOOOH; MMMMMEEEE; NNNNAAAA; NNNNOOOH; NNNEEE.
f. Practise the above combinations with a rising and falling pitch, i.e. start low, and make the voice climb as high as possible; start high and make the voice fall as low as possible. Use a full breath for these pitch exercises. Repeat each combination at least three times.
g. End on a loud shout, repeated five times, of the word TOPEKA!

These exercises should be done with the students standing in a circle. The exercises encourage awareness of breath control, without which there can be no voice control. Ask the students to tell you where they can 'feel' the vibrations created by the sounds. Exercise (f) might be visualized as in Figure 9.

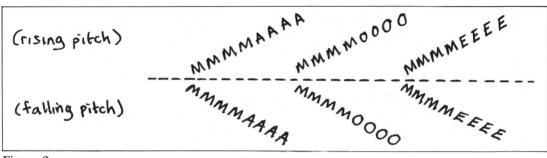

Figure 9

I would not recommend these exercises with very large classes, or groups for whom pitch and tone are not very serious problems.

Copying mouth-set

Start with 'face-loosening' exercises: widen the face as much as possible (eyes open wide, mouth gaping), then screw it up as tightly as possible. Next, place the palms of the hands on the cheeks and massage the face in different directions, pulling it up and down. End with head shaking, expelling air through loose lips ('blowing raspberries').

If you have video-recording facilities, you should film another teacher reading the guide to phonetic symbols printed at the front of the *Oxford Advanced Learner's Dictionary of Current English* (reprinted here in Table 2). During the filming, zoom in on the

<table>
<tr><td colspan="10">Phonetic symbols</td></tr>
<tr><td>Vowels and</td><td>1</td><td>iː</td><td>as in</td><td>see /siː/</td><td>11</td><td>ɜː</td><td>as in</td><td>fur /fɜː(r)/</td></tr>
<tr><td>Diphthongs</td><td>2</td><td>ɪ</td><td>as in</td><td>sit /sɪt/</td><td>12</td><td>ə</td><td>as in</td><td>ago /əˈgəʊ/</td></tr>
<tr><td></td><td>3</td><td>e</td><td>as in</td><td>ten /ten/</td><td>13</td><td>eɪ</td><td>as in</td><td>page /peɪdʒ/</td></tr>
<tr><td></td><td>4</td><td>æ</td><td>as in</td><td>hat /hæt/</td><td>14</td><td>əʊ</td><td>as in</td><td>home /həʊm/</td></tr>
<tr><td></td><td>5</td><td>ɑː</td><td>as in</td><td>arm /ɑːm/</td><td>15</td><td>aɪ</td><td>as in</td><td>five /faɪv/</td></tr>
<tr><td></td><td>6</td><td>ɒ</td><td>as in</td><td>got /gɒt/</td><td>16</td><td>aʊ</td><td>as in</td><td>now /naʊ/</td></tr>
<tr><td></td><td>7</td><td>ɔː</td><td>as in</td><td>saw /sɔː/</td><td>17</td><td>ɔɪ</td><td>as in</td><td>join /dʒɔɪn/</td></tr>
<tr><td></td><td>8</td><td>ʊ</td><td>as in</td><td>put /pʊt/</td><td>18</td><td>ɪə</td><td>as in</td><td>near /nɪə(r)/</td></tr>
<tr><td></td><td>9</td><td>uː</td><td>as in</td><td>too /tuː/</td><td>19</td><td>eə</td><td>as in</td><td>hair /heə(r)/</td></tr>
<tr><td></td><td>10</td><td>ʌ</td><td>as in</td><td>cup /kʌp/</td><td>20</td><td>ʊə</td><td>as in</td><td>pure /pjʊə(r)/</td></tr>
<tr><td>Consonants</td><td>1</td><td>p</td><td>as in</td><td>pen /pen/</td><td>13</td><td>s</td><td>as in</td><td>so /səʊ/</td></tr>
<tr><td></td><td>2</td><td>b</td><td>as in</td><td>bad /bæd/</td><td>14</td><td>z</td><td>as in</td><td>zoo /zuː/</td></tr>
<tr><td></td><td>3</td><td>t</td><td>as in</td><td>tea /tiː/</td><td>15</td><td>ʃ</td><td>as in</td><td>she /ʃiː/</td></tr>
<tr><td></td><td>4</td><td>d</td><td>as in</td><td>did /dɪd/</td><td>16</td><td>ʒ</td><td>as in</td><td>vision /ˈvɪʒn/</td></tr>
<tr><td></td><td>5</td><td>k</td><td>as in</td><td>cat /kæt/</td><td>17</td><td>h</td><td>as in</td><td>how /haʊ/</td></tr>
<tr><td></td><td>6</td><td>g</td><td>as in</td><td>got /gɒt/</td><td>18</td><td>m</td><td>as in</td><td>man /mæn/</td></tr>
<tr><td></td><td>7</td><td>tʃ</td><td>as in</td><td>chin /tʃɪn/</td><td>19</td><td>n</td><td>as in</td><td>no /nəʊ/</td></tr>
<tr><td></td><td>8</td><td>dʒ</td><td>as in</td><td>June /dʒuːn/</td><td>20</td><td>ŋ</td><td>as in</td><td>sing /sɪŋ/</td></tr>
<tr><td></td><td>9</td><td>f</td><td>as in</td><td>fall /fɔːl/</td><td>21</td><td>l</td><td>as in</td><td>lag /leg/</td></tr>
<tr><td></td><td>10</td><td>v</td><td>as in</td><td>voice /vɔɪs/</td><td>22</td><td>r</td><td>as in</td><td>red /red/</td></tr>
<tr><td></td><td>11</td><td>θ</td><td>as in</td><td>thin /θɪn/</td><td>23</td><td>j</td><td>as in</td><td>yes /jes/</td></tr>
<tr><td></td><td>12</td><td>ð</td><td>as in</td><td>then /ðen/</td><td>24</td><td>w</td><td>as in</td><td>wet /wet/</td></tr>
</table>

Table 2

teacher's mouth. In the classroom, freeze the picture of each sound, and get the students to imitate the shape of the teacher's mouth. Then show them the model word on a flash card. Practise these sounds in sets of five, and end with dialogues containing these key words.

The great advantage of the video is that once it is made, it can be used again and again, both for individual study and for classwork. The video that we produced at Stevenson College in Edinburgh shows a teacher holding flash cards with the key words of the sounds, and saying each of them three times, with the students joining in the third time. After each set of five sounds, the students were given a dialogue containing those key words for contextualized practice.

If you do not have video facilities, you have to be the model yourself. Allow the students to focus on the shape of your mouth, the position of your tongue, etc., and get them to bring mirrors to class to observe the different positions of their mouths.

It is very important to end with short dialogues which incorporate the words you have been practising, so as to give them context and meaning. Set the more advanced classes the task of creating dialogues containing these words.

Projecting clearly

Some students (depending on their cultural background) do not speak English loudly enough, which naturally hinders their communication. The following exercises are designed to encourage learners to project their voices clearly. Exercise (a) is also a valuable indication of individual success in copying mouth-set.

a. *Lip reading:* In pairs, students 'mouth' first words, then short sentences until their partners can understand what they are saying. Emphasize that they should make no sound, only use the shapes of their mouths to convey the message. You could give each student two words and two sentences on slips of paper, and get them to supply a third word and sentence themselves.

b. *Split dialogues:* Half the class have the initiations of different dialogues, the other half have the responses. The initiators have to say their parts loudly and clearly from one side of the room, so that the others on the other side can respond correctly. For example:

What's the time?
Nine o'clock.
It's Tuesday today.
That's right. (etc.)

c. *Throwing a poem around the class:* Each student has one line of a short poem or nursery rhyme (numbered to indicate its place in the sequence). They stand in different corners of the room. The teacher starts the poem, and each student responds where he or she should.

For example,

1 1–2–3–4
2 who's that knocking on my door?
3 5–6–7–8
4 birthday party don't be late
5 for the disco disco disco dancing
6 disco disco disco dancing.

(Circus of Poets: *OK Gimme – Poems for Children*)

  1 Hey look at me
  2 I'm a poet, poet
  3 I write about sheep
  4 So I know it, know it
  5 I write about sheep
  6 And I write about ducks
  7 Hens, Cows, Sheep, Ducks
  8 And I write them all down in my big new book
  9 I write them all down
10 And I read them all out
11 Ducks, Sheep, Hens, Cows,
12 This is what poetry's all about.

(John Turner: *Hard Shoulders Second Home*)

Learning rhythm

a. Group readings of easy poetry or nursery rhymes with a strong rhythmic beat that can be read as rounds (where two groups join at different times) lend themselves very well to the teaching of rhythm; for example,

Chewing chestnuts hurts my teeth
Chewing chestnuts hurts my teeth

It makes them crack and then fall out
It makes them crack and then fall out

And that's why I hate chestnuts
And that's why I hate chestnuts.

(Circus of Poets: *OK Gimme – Poems for Children*)

b. Some pop songs, especially those containing some lines that are 'spoken', will also provide students with an interesting and motivating way of learning rhythm. It is also a very satisfying way of ending a pronunciation lesson. Here are a few titles that I have exploited successfully in the past:

'We are the World' (USA for Africa)
'Yesterday' (The Beatles)
'Homeward Bound' (Simon and Garfunkel)
'The Boxer' (Simon and Garfunkel)
'I am a Rock' (Simon and Garfunkel)
'Hello, Goodbye' (The Beatles)
'Time after Time' (Cindy Lauper)

'I Just Called to Say I Loved You' (Stevie Wonder)
'That Old Devil Called Love' (Alison Moyet)
'Imagine' (John Lennon)

c. Sometimes individual sentences arise that create particular difficulty in terms of rhythm. Let the students say these sentences to a beat tapped or clapped out by you. If a piano is available, little tunes of four beats to a bar can also be used.

d. Finally, there is Carolyn Graham's excellent *Jazz Chants* (Oxford University Press, 1978), which very effectively combines the teaching of rhythm with other aspects of pronunciation, prosody, and structure.

Note
We cannot really isolate rhythm from any of the other aspects of pronunciation. While these methods are designed to sensitize students to the rhythm of English, the students also need good listening models that they should try to imitate as far as possible.

Group chanting/choral reading

The exercises in this section are also called 'vocal warm-ups'. They focus mainly on certain problem areas in English pronunciation, such as distinguishing between minimal pairs, the /dʒ/ sound for Spanish speakers, the /r/ /l/ distinction for Oriental learners, the /v/ /w/ distinction for German speakers, and so on. Each vocal warm-up should be repeated *five* times, with increasing speed and volume.

a. papapa/bababa/tatata/dadada/kakaka/gagaga.

b. The tip of the tongue, the teeth and the lips.

c. Hot coffee in a proper copper coffee pot.

d. Two flew through the window.

e. Who are you? Can't you see?

f. Make me many, many more.

g. Remember the money/Remember the money/Remember the money/Remember.

h. I'm pulling a long length of string.

i. She sells sea shells on the sea shore.

j. Look at the windmills whirling in the wind.

k. Julia Yeats will marry Judge Jeffreys in June.

l. The splendour falls on castle walls
And snowy summits old in story:
The long light shakes across the lakes,
And the wild cataract leaps in glory.
Blow, bugle, blow, set the wild echoes flying,
Blow, bugle; answer, echoes, dying, dying, dying.

(Tennyson)

(This should be done line by line, and then put together. It can also be read as a choral poem, with some lines given to the female voices and others to the male voices in the class.)

Note: 'Vocal warm-ups' should not be confused with warm-ups in general. This is the term used in the theatre for those exercises which help the actors to articulate clearly. Choose the ones that are relevant to your particular group, and follow them with more contextualized exercises like dialogues.

Stress and intonation

a. Give the students short scenes to read aloud in pairs. Use extracts from simplified plays or readers, or the more interesting coursebook dialogues. After practising their scenes, they should present them to the class, to see whether the class can understand what they are talking about. If they are not successful, you should help them, aided by the comments of the class as a whole, to improve on a second reading.

b. Prepare copies of the latest news (simplified for this level). Choose a few students to read it aloud to the class. Then explain why some were more successful than others.

c. Let the class listen to a short text on cassette. They should try to imitate the speaker exactly. Have a competition to see which student is the most successful mimic in the class, and then discuss why the others were less successful. A short poem can also be used in this way.

Note: At this level, it is advisable to mark the stressed words and syllables, to make the reading easier for your students. The stressed sections can also be written in capital letters, e.g. 'I want to call him NOW, not LAter'. Intonation patterns should also be marked, particularly in the case of Oriental students; for example:

Why is he looking so cross ?

Why is he looking so CROSS?

Figure 10

Teaching pronunciation and prosody to intermediate students

All the exercises recommended for use with beginner and elementary students can also be used with intermediate students. Here are some more challenging vocal warm-ups and choral poetry to be used at this level. They should be repeated five times with increasing speed and volume.

a. In Tooting two tutors astute
tried to toot to a Duke on a flute
but duets so gruelling
end only in duelling
when tutors astute toot the flute.

b. For the moon never beams
without bringing me dreams
of the beautiful Annabelle Lee.

(Edgar Allan Poe)

c. Literary secretaries are fortunately a rarity.

d. Contemporary literature literally littered the library table.

e. This particularly rapid, unintelligible patter
Isn't generally heard, and if it is, it doesn't matter.

(W.S. Gilbert)

f. Willows whiten, aspens quiver,
Little breezes dusk and shiver.

(Alfred Lord Tennyson)

g. Whether the weather is cold
Whether the weather is hot
We'll weather the weather
Whatever the weather
Whether we like it or not!

h. Yesterday is just a memory,
Tomorrow, only a dream.
Let's live just for today.

For practice in stress and intonation at this level, you can use extracts from unsimplified plays, such as the ones recommended in Chapter 8. The students can also be asked to memorize a short reading passage, and to prepare individual talks. These can then be recorded for feedback.

Teaching pronunciation and prosody to upper-intermediate and advanced students

Students at this level need plenty of opportunity for reading aloud, and listening to their own voices on tape. The biggest problem at this level is not the pronunciation of individual words, but intonation, stress, and rhythm – problems that they are often not even aware of. Again, many of the exercises previously presented can be used at this level, and also the following vocal warm-ups and poetry extracts:

a. Great rats, small rats, lean rats, brawny rats,
   Brown rats, black rats, grey rats, tawny rats,
   Grave old plodders, gay young friskers,
   Fathers, mothers, uncles, cousins,
   Cocking tails and pricking whiskers,
   Families by tens and dozens,
   Brothers, sisters, husbands, wives,
   Followed the piper for their lives.
   (Robert Browning)

b. How sweet the moonlight sleeps upon this bank!
   Here will we sit, and let the sounds of music
   Creep into our ears.
   (Shakespeare)

c. Very well, Sir Winston:
   We'll wed on Wednesday
   if you buy me that very white vase.

d. Articulatory agility
   Is a desired ability,
   Manipulating with dexterity
   The tongue, the palate and the lips.

e. I am the very model of a modern Major-General.
   I've information vegetable, animal and mineral.
   I know the Kings of England, and I quote the fights historical
   From Marathon to Waterloo, in order categorical.
   I'm very well acquainted too with matters mathematical,
   I understand equations, both the simple and quadratical.
   About binomial theorem I'm teeming with a lot o' news –
   With many cheerful facts about the square of the hypotenuse.
   I'm very good at integral and differential calculus,
   I know the scientific names of beings animalculous;
   In short, in matters vegetable, animal and mineral,
   I am the very model of a modern Major-General.

(W.S. Gilbert)

For stress and intonation practice, students at this level can also do dramatized playreadings, either in pairs or groups, which can be recorded for feedback. They could also listen to extracts from radio plays, and then try to copy the speakers' models. The BBC publishes its radio plays, so it is possible to get the exact scripts of the plays. Singing, individual talks with feedback and, where possible, regular practice with native speakers, will all assist the learner in improving pronunciation and prosody in English.

References and recommended reading

Circus of Poets. 1985. *OK GIMME – Poems for Children.* Rotherham: Versewagon Press.

Honikman, Beatrice. 1964. 'Articulatory settings' in *In Honour of Daniel Jones*. London: Longmans, Green.

Smith, Stephen M. 1984. *The Theatre Arts and the Teaching of Second Languages*. London: Addison–Wesley.

Turner, John. 1983. *Hard Shoulders Second Home*. Rotherham: Versewagon Press.

Turner, J. Clifford. 1950. *Voice and Speech in the Theatre* (revised by Malcolm Morrison). London: A. & C. Black.

5 Using drama to teach spoken communication skills

Introduction

The purpose of this chapter is to show how lessons based on drama, such as dramatized play readings with extension activities, improvisations, situational role plays, and video can be added to your existing repertoire of spoken communication activities. But although these lessons are presented as another category of spoken communicaton activities, I would like to emphasize that drama has a role to play in the success of all group activities, because the use of drama games and warm-ups can contribute significantly to good group dynamics. None of these activities will work unless the students have accepted each other as people and are willing to co-operate with each other (see Chapter 1).

Many of the games presented in Chapter 2, particularly the 'Starters', are excellent preparatory activities. Even the longer vocal warm-ups of Chapter 4 can serve as 'ice-breakers' before the main activities start, especially if the group appears listless or bored.

Ideally, a session on spoken communication skills should have the following outline:

a. Warm-up (game or chant):   5 minutes
b. Explaining the main activity: 5 minutes
c. Main activity: 30–45 minutes
d. Feedback: 10–30 minutes

Where necessary, the game should reflect the main activity, but this is not a rigid rule.Its main purpose is to relax the learners, sharpen their concentration, and stimulate their imagination.

For example, as a warm-up activity to introduce a role play called 'The Lonely Hearts Column' (in *Act English*, by Peter Watcyn-Jones), we played the game 'Find your partner', while the vocal warm-up 'A modern major-general' was sufficient to enliven the class for an improvisation called 'Hot off the press' (described later in this chapter). I have also used songs and jazz chants as warm-up activities, and (very occasionally!) physical warm-ups.

Dramatized play readings with extension activities

There are many books currently available which contain plays and sketches specially written for language teaching, for example *Off-Stage!* by Doug Case and Ken Wilson. (An approach to one of the sketches in *Off-Stage!* is described in Chapter 6.) But there is no reason why you should not use extracts from original, unsimplified plays, as the language of these extracts will be so much richer and more unrestricted than the simplified sketches. In choosing your texts, many of the criteria set out at the beginning of Chapter 8 will apply, the exceptions being that for classwork you need not restrict your genres (melodramas can also be used, and symbolic and 'absurd' plays), and you can use scenes calling for as few as two characters. The extracts used should not exceed the length of an A4 sheet, depending on the level of the class. The scene chosen should also be able to stand on its own as a meaningful unit. Here are five approaches to scene-work:

1 Choose a text with very simple vocabulary and short utterances. Give each student a copy, and read it aloud to them. Ask them a few comprehension questions, and then encourage them to speculate about the context of the scene – what preceded it, and what will follow? Then divide the class into groups according to the number of characters in the scene. They now practise reading the scene aloud, using Michael West's read-and-look-up method. They should look at their lines briefly, and then look up when they say them. As a follow-up activity, they can be asked to improvise continuations of the scene.

Notes
I have used this technique with elementary and pre-intermediate students. They find the read-and-look-up method very challenging, and often succeed in memorizing their lines by the end of the session. Difficulties in vocabulary and pronunciation are dealt with after the first reading by the teacher, and also during the groupwork. For this lesson, the following extract from David Campton's *Us and Them* works well:

A1 Here?
B1 Here.
A1 It's a good place.
B1 Yes, it's a good place.
A2 Better than any other place we've seen.
B2 It's a good place all right.
A1 To pause at.
B1 To stay at.
A2 To make our own.

B2 For ever and ever.
A1 This is our place.
B1 Ours.
A2 Ours.
B2 We took long enough to find it.
A3 It was a long journey.
B3 But it was worth every day we searched.
A1 It was worth every mile we tramped.
B1 Look at it.
A2 Just look.
B2 Look here.
A3 Look there.
B3 Look.
A1 Look.

(from *Double Act*, ed. M. Shackleton, 1985)

2 Give the class copies of a scene from which all the stage directions have been deleted. Tell them that they are a team of directors and have to decide how the scene should be played by the actors. Then divide the class into groups, and let them work out the stage directions: how the lines should be said and what movements and facial expressions should accompany the acting. It would be most useful to write a number of adverbs of feeling on the board, but also encourage students to use dictionaries. The groups can then compare and contrast their different interpretations until the whole class agrees on a single set of stage directions. The session can end with a dramatized playreading by selected students or volunteers. This can be recorded for feedback.

Notes
This activity works well with students at the intermediate to advanced levels. Since the main focus is the discussion of how the lines should be said, even those students who dislike reading aloud can become actively involved. They will also be encouraged to think critically of such factors as intonation, stress, and rhythm when they try out different ways of saying the lines. In addition, it is rare for a group to agree unanimously on the interpretation, and this ensures that the discussion is kept going. Harold Pinter's *Trouble in the Works* and *A Slight Ache* are examples of plays that can be used for this activity, as well as the following extract from Peter Shaffer's *The Private Ear*:

Bob: I'm sorry. (*He switches off the gramophone.*)
Doreen: That's all right.
Bob: No, no, it isn't. It isn't at all. (*Long pause*) Actually, you see, I've brought you here under false pretences. I should never have asked you. You see, I didn't really tell you everything about myself. That was wrong of me. Please forgive me.

Doreen: What d'you mean?

Bob: Well, you see, actually I'm engaged.

Doreen: Engaged?

Bob: Yes. To be married.

Doreen: (*Really surprised*): *You* are?

Bob: (*Defiantly*): Yes. Yes. So I shouldn't have asked you here. I'm sorry. (*She stares at him. He is not looking at her. On a sudden impulse he picks up the photograph of the girl left by Ted.*)

Doreen: Is that her?

Bob: Yes.

Doreen: Can I see? (*He passes it to her.*) She looks lovely.

Bob: Yes, she is, very. That's really raven black, her hair. It's got tints of blue in it. You can't really judge from a photo.

Doreen: What's her name?

Bob: Er . . . Lavinia. It's rather an unusual name, isn't it? Lavinia. I think it's rather distinguished.

Doreen: Yes, it is.

Bob: Like her. She's distinguished. She's got a way with her. Style, you know. It's what they used to call carriage. (*She gives him a startled look.*) So you see . . . well – no harm done, I suppose.

Doreen: (*Dully*): No, of course not.

Bob: Here's your coat. (*He helps her with it. She is hardly listening to him.*) I wonder why I thought an ocelot was a bird. I wasn't thinking of an ostrich. It was those pictures you see of ladies in Edwardian photos with long, traily feathers in their hats. Is there such a thing as an osprey?

Doreen: I wouldn't know. (*With a smile*) It's not really ocelot, you know. It's lamb dyed. And it's not really cold enough for fur coats anyway, is it, yet? I was showing off.

Bob: I'm glad you did.

(*They go to the door.*)

Doreen: Well, it's been lovely.

Bob: For me, too.

Doreen: I enjoyed the music. Really.

Bob: Good.

Doreen: Perhaps we'll meet again. At a concert or somewhere.

Bob: Yes. Perhaps we will.

Doreen: I'm glad about your girl. She looks lovely.

Bob: She is.

(*They avoid each other's look.*)

Doreen: Well, good night.

Bob: Good night.

(from *Peter Shaffer – Four Plays*, Penguin 1981)

3 Take one scene and split it into three or four coherent sections. Give each section to a different group or pair. They should first decide how the lines should be said, and should write their stage directions on their scripts. They should also attempt to analyse the characters in the scene – how do these characters behave towards the other characters, and how are they treated by them? Next, they should rehearse their sections in different corners of the room (each group can appoint its own director). When they are ready, put the whole scene together in its correct sequence and let each group act out its own section. Then have a discussion about the different interpretations of the same characters (as different students will have portrayed the same character). As a follow-up activity, put the students who have portrayed the same character in one group, and let them write a personality profile of the character.

Notes
The most important aspect of this activity is the actual text you select, especially if you are teaching large classes. You will need a scene with more than two characters, and these characters should not be too easy to analyse (in other words, they could be acted in different ways). Plays that can be good sources for this activity include Samuel Becket's *Waiting for Godot*, Harold Pinter's *The Birthday Party*, Agatha Christie's *The Patient*, and Alan Ayckbourn's *Absent Friends*. This activity works well with upper-intermediate and advanced students.

4 Choose four short scenes with a common theme, for example *relationships*. Give these scenes to different groups or pairs, depending on the number of characters in each scene. Let each group discuss its own scene – what it means, its context, the relationships of the characters, and how they think the scene should be interpreted. Help them where necessary with the vocabulary and the pronunciation. When they have completed this stage, tell each group to choose a director within the group. They should then practise acting out the scene under the leadership of the director. When each group is ready, they should present their dramatizations to the rest of the class as follows:

a. The director gives a brief summary of the scene.

b. The group act it out.

c. The audience suggest ways in which the scene could continue. (This can be done either in a quick 'brainstorming' session, or in group discussions.)

d. The group select the best ideas for continuation.

When each group has presented its scene in this way, give them five or ten minutes to improvise a continuation which will add two minutes to their scene. They then act out their original scene, followed by the continuation, which can then be assessed and criticized by the other groups.

Notes

This activity, which is intended for upper-intermediate and
advanced students, may need more than one session, although it
can lose its vitality and sense of immediacy if split up in this way.
Ideally, a session lasting two hours should be devoted to it.

Here are four short scenes (from *Contemporary Scenes for Student
Actors*, ed. Schulman and Mackler, 1980) that can be used for the
theme 'Relationships'.

a. From Scene 2 of *Lovers and Other Strangers* by Renée Taylor and
Joseph Bologna

He, *sits*: You want to know why you're so confused? Because you
   forgot who I am and who you are. I'm the man and you're just the
   woman, and the man is the boss. You said so yourself when we got
   married.
She: I was just humouring you. I said, 'If it was so important to
   you, I would let you be the boss.'
He: What do you mean, 'Let me be the boss'? I am the boss.
She: Don't be juvenile. There is no boss.
He: I am the boss and you know it.
She: There is no boss and that's final. I don't want to hear another
   word about it. We are equals. *Sits on bed.*
He, *his frustration is building*: Oh, we're equal, huh? *Standing up on
   bed.*
She: Yes! We're equal.
He: All right, let's just see how equal we are. *Pulls her up.* Come
   on, equal. Let's go a couple of rounds.
She: Cut it out, you big jerk! *He dazzles her with his footwork. She
   punches him in stomach and tries to run away from him. He catches
   her. He grabs her arms and holds them behind her back. She can't
   move. She struggles to get free, but he is too strong for her.* Let me go.
He: You're my equal. Why don't you let yourself go?
She: Stop it.
He: Who's the boss?

b. From Act I of *Thieves* by Herb Gardner

Sally: Can I ask you a question?
Martin: Yes.
Sally: Who are you?
Martin: Martin.
Sally, *thoughtfully*: Martin, Martin . . .
Martin: Martin Cramer.
Sally: Martin Cramer. Right. *After a moment:* And where do I
   know you from?
Martin: I'm your husband. You know me from marriage.
Sally, *nodding*: Right, right . . .
Martin, *opening his eyes*: Sally, the forgetting game. I hate it. You
   have no idea how much I hate it.

Sally: OK, OK, I—

Martin, *sitting up at edge of bed*: Sally, at least once a week now you wake me up in the middle of the night and ask me who I am. I hate it.

Sally: You used to think it was charming.

c. From Act III of *Play It Again, Sam* by Woody Allen

Allan: Gee, I can't believe it. This bright, beautiful woman is in love with me. Of course she's in love with me. Why shouldn't she be? I'm bright, amusing . . . sensitive face . . . fantastic body. Dick'll understand. Hell, we're two civilized guys. In the course of our social encounters a little romance has developed. It's a very natural thing to happen amongst sophisticated people.

Dick, *appearing in dream light:* You sent for me?

Allan: Yes

Dick: Good.

Allan: Drink?

Dick: Quite.

Allan: Scotch?

Dick: Fine.

Allan: Neat?

Dick: Please.

Allan: Soda?

Dick: A dash.

Allan: Linda and I are in love.

Dick: It's just as well. I've come from my doctor. He gives me two months to live.

d. From Scene 10 of *A Streetcar Named Desire* by Tennessee Williams

Stanley: Yep. Just me and you, Blanche. Unless you got somebody hid under the bed. What've you got on those fine feathers for?

Blanche: Oh, that's right. You left before my wire came.

Stanley: You got a wire?

Blanche: I received a telegram from an old admirer of mine.

Stanley: Anything good?

Blanche: I think so. An invitation.

Stanley: What to? A fireman's ball?

Blanche, *throwing back her head*: A cruise of the Caribbean on a yacht!

Stanley: Well, well. What do you know?

Blanche: I have never been so suprised in my life.

Stanley: I guess not.

Blanche: It came like a bolt from the blue!

Stanley: Who did you say it was from?

Blanche: An old beau of mine.

A detailed lesson, based on an extract from a play by Agatha Christie

Extract from *The Patient*, by Agatha Christie, in *Twenty One-Act Plays: An Anthology for Amateur Performing Groups* ed. Stanley, 1978:

Emmeline: There's not much doubt is there, who she meant? 'B.' (*She looks at Wingfield.*) Not much doubt about that, is there, Bryan?

Wingfield: You always hated me, Emmeline. You always had it in for me. I tell you here and now, I didn't try to kill my wife.

Emmeline: Do you deny that you were having an affair with that woman there? (*She points at Brenda.*)

Brenda: (*Rising*) It's not true.

Emmeline: Don't tell me that. You were head over ears in love with him.

Brenda: (*Facing the others*) All right, then. I *was* in love with him. But that was all over ages ago. He didn't really care for me. It's all over, I tell you. All over!

Emmeline: In that case it seems odd you stayed on as his secretary.

Brenda: I didn't want to go. I – oh, all right, then! (*Passionately*) I still wanted to be near him. (*She sits.*)

Emmeline: And perhaps you thought that if Jenny were out of the way, you'd console him very nicely, and be Mrs Wingfield Number Two . . .

Wingfield: Emmeline, for heaven's sake!

Emmeline: Perhaps it's 'B' for Brenda.

Brenda: You horrible woman! I hate you. It's not true.

Ross: (*Rising*) Bryan – and Brenda. It seems to narrow it down to one of you two all right.

Wingfield: I wouldn't say that. It could be 'B' for brother, couldn't it? Or Bill?

Ross: She always called me William.

Wingfield: After all, who stands to gain by poor Jenny's death? Not me. It's you. You and Emmeline. It's you two who'll get her money.

Ginsberg: Please – please! I can't have all this argument. Nurse, will you take them down to the waiting room.

Nurse: Yes, Doctor.

Ross: (*Turning to Ginsberg*) We can't stay cooped up in a little room with all of us slanging each other.

Inspector: You can go where you please on the hospital premises, but none of you is actually to leave the place. (*Sharply*) Is that understood?

Wingfield: All right.

Ross: Yes.

Emmeline: I have no wish to leave. My conscience is clear.

Brenda: (*Going up to her*) I think – *you* did it.

Emmeline: (*Sharply*) What do you mean?

Brenda: You hate her – you've always hated her. And you get the money – you and your brother.

Emmeline: My name does not begin with a 'B', I'm thankful to say.

Brenda: (*Excitedly*) No – but it needn't. (*She turns to the Inspector.*) Supposing that, after all, Mrs Wingfield *didn't* see who it was who pushed her off the balcony.

Emmeline: She has told us that she did.

Brenda: But supposing that she didn't. (*Crosses to the Inspector*) Don't you see what a temptation it might be to her? She was jealous of me and Bryan – oh, yes, she knew about us – and she was jealous. And when that machine there (*she gestures towards the electrical apparatus*) gave her a chance to get back at us – at me – don't you see how tempting it was to say 'Brenda pushed me . . .'? It could have been like that, it could!

Inspector: A little far-fetched.

Brenda: No, it isn't! Not to a jealous woman. You don't know what women are like when they're jealous. And she'd been cooped up there in her room – thinking – suspecting – wondering if Bryan and I were still carrying on together. It isn't far-fetched, I tell you. It could easily be true. (*She looks at Wingfield.*)

Wingfield: It's quite possible, you know, Inspector.

Brenda: (*To Emmeline*) And you *do* hate her.

Emmeline: Me? My own sister?

Brenda: I've seen you looking at her often. You were in love with Bryan – he was half engaged to you – and then Jenny came home from abroad and cut you out. (*Facing Emmeline*) Oh, she told me the whole story one day. You've never forgiven her. I think you've hated her ever since. I think that you came into her room that day, and you saw her leaning over the balcony, and it was too good a chance to be missed – you came up behind her and (*With a gesture*) pushed her over . . .

IN CLASS

Stage One

Warm-up. Play the game 'Whodunnit?' (Chapter 2)

Stage Two

Introductory discussion, using the following questions:

1 Do you know about the works of Agatha Christie? Have you read any of them?

2 Have you seen any films of her books, like *Murder on the Orient Express*?

3 What is the most striking thing about her murder mysteries?

(Note: If they do not know the answers, briefly tell them about Agatha Christie's works.)

Stage Three

Listening comprehension, using a recording of native speakers reading a scene from the *The Patient*. The following questions are asked:

1 Where does this scene take place?
2 How many characters are involved?
3 Who is the victim?
4 What possible motive could each of the following characters have for wanting to kill the victim: Bryan, Brenda, Bill, and Emmeline?

(Note: this stage is optional, depending on the level of the group and the availability of native speakers.)

Stage Four

Silent reading of the scene, and explanation of vocabulary.

Stage Five

Dramatizations. The class is divided into groups. Each group appoints a director. They then work on a dramatization of the scene, using such props as are available in the classroom. Each group's dramatization is then presented to the class for criticism. The director of each group takes note of all the criticisms, and the groups then try to improve on their first attempt.

Stage Six

Feedback. The teacher, who should have ample time during Stage Five to note errors, can now issue feedback sheets to individual students, or discuss persistent errors with the class as a whole. If any recordings have been made, these can now be played back to the class and analysed.

FOLLOW-UP

1 Discussion:

a. Analyse the personalities of each character.

b. Who do you think tried to kill the victim? Give reasons for your choice.

c. Why is the letter 'B' so significant?

d. What do you think preceded this scene?

e. How do you think the scene will continue?

2 Writing and role play:

In groups, the students write a five-minute continuation of this scene, and then act out their new scenes to the class. It would be good if you could record or film them. Finally, give the class the actual continuation of the scene, for comparison and discussion.

Improvisations

The primacy of improvisation in classes dealing with spoken communication skills can clearly be seen in many of the lessons presented in this chapter, and indeed in the book as a whole. Improvisation taps the students' already existing command of the language and tests their communicative strategies. Some of the games presented in Chapter 2 are, in fact, improvisations, and can be extended into fuller versions for spoken communication skills lessons. Examples are: 'Every picture tells a story', 'Moving picture', 'Us and them', 'Alibi', and 'Puppet on a string'.

The improvisations presented here can be used on their own, with another improvisation, or in combination with a selection of games and other communication activities. Careful preparation of the group is essential, as even native speakers can find improvisation quite daunting without adequate warm-up activities. These warm-up activities can include the following:

- re-arrangement of the furniture in the room (students should preferably be seated in a circle, away from their desks, and can even sit on the floor);
- physical warm-ups (optional);
- non-verbal games like 'Cup ball', 'The trust circle', and 'Mirrors';
- verbal games like 'Feelings', 'Concentration', and 'Robot'.

Brainstorming play
For intermediate to advanced students

This involves building up a short scene from one word or picture. The class is divided into four groups, and each group is given the same word or picture. They are given ten minutes to devise a scene based on it. If necessary, they can note down some of their ideas, but they should preferably do the improvisation without written prompts. They then perform their scene to the class, and after all the scenes have been performed, the teacher can give feedback on each scene. As a follow-up activity, the students can write out the whole scene. Here is an example of a scene devised by one group of students. The key word was *don't!*

A: Don't!

B: I must. Don't try to stop me.

A: Please, *listen* to me.

B: NO! It's too late, I tell you!

A: But what will happen to your children? And what about me?

B: I don't care! Get out of my way!

A: (*pulls out a gun*) You're going nowhere. (*takes aim*)

B: What??? You silly fool – can't you see what I'm trying to do? If you shoot me, it will be murder!

A: I know.

B: All I want is a nice quiet suicide. I want to jump from this ledge. I want to do it my way, but not your way. You know I hate guns!

A: Yes, I know. (*takes aim again*) So — what are you going to do?

B: Well . . . I'll just come in for a bit, and have a cup of tea with you.

A: And we'll talk about all your problems, OK?

B: OK.

Other words that have elicited a good response are: *what?*, *rubbish!*, *whisky*, *really?*, *quite*, *liar!*, *camera*, and *storm*. If you use pictures, they should show people doing various things. The scenes produced by the students should be approximately two minutes long.

Music-picture
For elementary to advanced students

Play some instrumental music to the students. The music should be suggestive of a variety of things, for example running water, birds, or the wind. The students should listen to it with their eyes shut, and try to picture the scene which the music suggests. Play the music twice. In groups, the students then discuss what they visualized while listening to the music. They then devise a mime to accompany the music. Their mime should incorporate all the elements they discussed in their groups. Each group then performs their mime to the rest of the class, who should try to guess what the mime means. Sound-tracks from films, for example the theme from *ET*, can be used for this activity.

Hot off the press
For intermediate and advanced students

Choose newspaper articles about famous personalities. Students sit in pairs, and read an article. You can move around the class, giving assistance with difficult vocabulary. The students then improvise the interview between the famous person and the reporter who wrote the article. This improvised interview is then presented to the class, using the typical 'chat-show' format. You can make a tape recording or video for feedback.

The go-between
For intermediate and advanced students

One half of the class is a group of terrorists, who are threatening to blow up the class/school/building (or any important installation) unless their demands are met. The other half is a group of officials trying to negotiate with them. One person, chosen by both groups, acts as the go-between. S/he reports the words of one group to the other. The dialogue starts with the officials asking 'What do you want?' The go-between's task is to report to both sides as accurately as possible, or the negotiations will fall through. They have to try to come to a satisfactory agreement within fifteen minutes.

Yes/No
For intermediate and advanced students

Tell the class that you have an interesting story to tell them, but that they will hear only the introduction. To find out the rest of the story, they should ask you questions that can be answered only with 'yes' or 'no'. When you have introduced the story, let the questioning begin. Now you simply apply the technique of answering 'yes' to all questions ending in vowels, and 'no' to all questions ending in consonants. In this way, the students actually build up the whole story without being aware of it. Halt the questioning occasionally, and either give them a summary of the story so far yourself, or get one of them to sum up. This improvisation works particularly well with shy, inhibited students, as it arouses their curiosity and forces them to ask questions. Here is an example of the type of introduction that can be used, and the questions provoked by it:

The scene is a room decorated and laid out for a party. It is nine o'clock at night. There are four people in the room – two men and two women. They are all holding glasses of wine. The people are silent, and they are all staring intently at something . . . Can you guess why they are silent, what they are staring at, and how the story will continue?

Has there been a fight? No.
Has a stranger come in? — No.
Are they staring at a picture? — Yes.
Is the picture of one of them? — No.
Is the picture pretty? — Yes.
Is the picture of a young lady? — Yes.
Is she dead? — No.
Is she alive? — Yes.
Is she coming to the party? — Yes.
Is she late? — Yes.
Are they worried? — No.
Are they angry? — Yes.
etc.

The questions can go on until you decide to call a halt. It is advisable, particularly with weaker classes, to write the openings of some questions on the board, for example:

Is . . . ?
Are they . . . ?
Has there . . . ?
Have they . . . ?
Will she/he/they . . . ?
Did . . . ?

Situational role plays

As the name suggests, situational role plays deal with situations that are likely to occur to the learner in his or her daily life. If you are teaching in the UK or any other English-speaking country, you will find that these situational role plays are similar to those used in the teaching of English to immigrants (ESL), and it would therefore be worthwhile to invest in some of these materials. Suzanne Hayes's *Drama as a Second Language* contains many relevant and interesting role plays for ESL students, which she calls role-simulations.

Situational role plays rely heavily on the skill of improvisation, as well as what Dorothy Heathcote calls 'teaching in role'; this means that you, the teacher, assume a variety of roles to challenge and interact with the learners. This is especially pertinent if you are the only native speaker present, but if team-teaching is a possibility, a second teacher could direct the proceedings.

Situational role plays in the UK: an example

The example given below was based on a real-life situation confronting a few part-time students of mine who worked as waiters in a hotel. A rule of the hotel was that they were not allowed to eat any of the food left over on the tables after the guests had gone. One of them was very hungry, however, and was caught eating a potato by the rather vindictive head-waiter. When the unfortunate culprit was reported to the manager, he was sacked. The other waiters then decided to go on strike, so the management decided to call a meeting to sort out the crisis. The role play is based on this meeting.

```
ROLE CARD A

You are Pierre, and you have been sacked
for eating a left-over potato.  At all the
other hotels where you have worked before,
you were allowed to eat left-over food.
You feel very bitter about the sacking, as
you have worked hard and are popular with
the guests at the hotel.  You feel that the
head-waiter is jealous of your popularity
and dislikes French people.  Explain your
side of the situation to the manager.
```

Photocopiable © Oxford University Press

ROLE CARD B

You are Richard, the head-waiter. You have
been told to enforce the rule about left-over
food strictly. You don't particularly like
the foreign waiters under your control, as
you feel that they are over-familiar with
the guests, and will steal food whenever they
get the chance. Explain your side of the
situation to the manager.

ROLE CARD C

You are Mr Mackay, the manager. You have
sacked Pierre for breaking a hotel rule.
But now the other waiters are threatening
to strike, the hotel is full of guests, and
two wedding receptions and a major conference
are booked for the weekend. You want to
take Pierre back, but you don't want to
appear weak or to undermine Richard's
authority. The final solution rests with
you.

ROLE CARD D

You are Michel, and you represent the rest
of the waiters. You see Pierre's case as
an excellent opportunity to bring all the
other other grievances of the waiters to
the manager's attention: the long hours,
the low pay, and the repressive atmosphere.
You dislike Richard intensely, and believe
that he should be replaced with someone
more friendly. Explain your side of the
situation to the manager.

In this role play, the students were first allowed to familiarize themselves with their roles, and were encouraged to think about the age, status, background, and personality of the person they were playing. The role play then started (in groups of four), and after about fifteen minutes, I started to teach in role by taking over one role in each group, spending approximately five minutes with each group before moving on to the next group. This revitalized the role play, and provided the students with some interaction with a native speaker. The class found the role play very relevant and informative, and began to put forward more situations that actually mattered to them. In this way I was able to 'structure for a learning situation to happen rather than for a sharing of information in a "final" way to take place' (to use Dorothy Heathcote's words).

Situational role plays for EFL students in other countries: some ideas

It is also possible to create situational role plays for EFL students in other countries, by examining situations where the students are likely to interact with English-speaking people in their own countries. Here are some ideas:

```
An English-speaking family has moved in next
door to your family.  Your parents speak no
English, so you have to act as interpreter
every time your parents need to speak to them.
Here are some ideas for role plays:

1   Invite them to dinner.
2   Tell them about the neighbourhood, the
    nearest shops, the bus stops, the parks, etc.
3   They want to borrow some of your father's
    tools.  Improvise the dialogue.
4   You discover that your mother has fallen and
    broken her hip while your father is away.
    You run to the neighbours for help.
5   Your mother, who plays the piano, is worried
    that the noise could be disturbing the
    neighbours.  You are sent to enquire whether
    this is so.  The lady of the house doesn't
    seem to mind, but her husband clearly does.
    You agree on a more convenient time for
    your mother to practise.
```

You decide to study in a language school in
Britain. Role play these situations:

1 Telephone the school in London to get
   details of the course, how much it will
   cost, whether accommodation is arranged, etc.
2 While travelling to Britain, you make
   friends with an English-speaking fellow-
   passenger. Improvise your conversation.
3 Owing to a misunderstanding, the British
   family who were to meet you at the airport
   have not yet arrived. You telephone their
   house, and their son tells you that they are
   on their way. Role play this conversation.
4 On your first day at the school, you
   accidentally join the wrong class. After
   a few minutes, you realize your mistake.
   Explain your problem to the teacher.
5 You are unhappy with your accommodation and
   would like to change it. Discuss the problem
   with the school's accommodation officer.

Photocopiable © Oxford University Press

Note: As most situational role plays are prepared by the teacher in
accordance with the needs of the group, they can be adapted to suit
a range of levels. Essential vocabulary and structures should be
supplied, and practice in using the correct registers in different
situations is also important. (See the list of source books at the end
of this book.)

The use of video

Apart from filming students for feedback, there are a number of
ways in which video can aid the use of drama in language teaching.
This is how I have exploited it in the past:

1 Students watch a short scene from a play, with the sound turned
down. They then improvise the dialogue, and finally compare and
contrast their dialogues with the original one.

2 Students watch a newsreader reading a news summary. After
watching this twice, they are given copies of the news, and asked to
mimic the newsreader – not just his or her reading of the news, but
also facial expressions, mannerisms, and gestures. The student who
is the best mimic is declared the winner, and the class then discuss
why she or he was more successful than the others.

3 Using the BBC's 'Speakeasy' video, a set of fifteen mime sketches, students have to produce the dialogue for the sketches themselves, and then role play the situations. The video is accompanied by a student's and a teacher's book, and can be used at most levels except beginners.

4 The students devise their own script for a documentary or drama. They then film it themselves, after receiving instructions on how to use the equipment. If hand-held cameras are available, the students could also film outside the school. This would, of course, be a full-scale project, which needs to be developed over a number of weeks.

5 The students devise a pop video to accompany a pop song – an activity that functions on the same principles of visualization as the improvisation 'Music picture', described earlier in this chapter.

Note: Apart from activity (3), these work best with upper-intermediate and advanced students.

References and recommended reading

Case, D. and **K. Wilson.** 1978. *Off Stage!* London: Heinemann.

Gow, Marion. 1982. *The Commercial Scene: Role Playing for Commerce Students.* London: Edward Arnold.

Hayes, Suzanne. 1984. *Drama as a Second Language.* Cambridge: National Extension College.

Nicholson, Richard. 1978. *Open to Question – Starters for Discussion and Role Play.* London: Edward Arnold.

Revell, Jane. 1979. *Teaching Techniques for Communicative English.* London: Macmillan.

Schulman and **Meckler** (eds.) 1980. *Contemporary Scenes for Student Actors.* New York: Penguin.

Shackleton, Mark (ed.) 1985. *Double Act.* London: Edward Arnold.

Spaventa, Lou (ed.) 1980. *Towards the Creative Teaching of English.* London: Allen and Unwin.

Stanley, Susan. 1980. *Drama Without Script.* London: Hodder and Stoughton.

Walker, David. 1979, 1982, 1983. *Dilemmas 1, 2* and *3.* London: Edward Arnold.

Walker, David. 1981. *Kith and Kin.* London: Edward Arnold.

Watcyn-Jones, Peter. 1978. *Act English.* London: Penguin.

6 Drama in the teaching of literature

Introduction

Literature is currently enjoying a welcome revival in TEFL at the upper-intermediate and advanced levels. Teachers at these levels realize the importance of teaching their students the subtleties of English idiom and register, and literature is a rich source of these features. In writing this chapter, I am much influenced by the work of Dorothy Heathcote, one of the world's leading authorities on drama in education. Heathcote believes that too much time is spent by teachers on critical analysis of literature, and not nearly enough on 'the universality of all human experience'. Students are rarely allowed to view a text as anything but an abstract, flat piece of printed matter, isolated from and irrelevant to their lives. Thus they never really enter into the text or believe in the characters' lives and motivations.

While basic text analysis to make clear the writer's use of the language cannot be omitted from the teaching of literature, the task of the teacher will be greatly simplified if the students can be allowed to identify with the characters in the book, and can see them as real people with real dilemmas. In other words, the teacher needs to make the text 'stand up and walk about'. And this is where drama comes in, not simply in the dramatized reading of some sections of the book, but also as a means of helping the students to 'see beyond' the printed page.

The key notions underlying my approach to the four works of literature presented here are:

- creating a need for action
- infusing dramatic tension
- stepping into role
- seeing beyond the immediate
- slowing down the experience
- encouraging students to take decisions.

These notions correspond closely with Dorothy Heathcote's treatment of text. The works I have chosen are a one-act play by James Saunders, *Over the Wall*; a novel by Alan Paton, *Cry, the Beloved Country*; a poem by Walter de la Mare, 'The Listeners'; and a simplified work: 'The Ticket Inspector' (from Doug Case and Ken Wilson's *Off-Stage!*). *Over The Wall* will be treated in most detail, to illustrate the basic pattern, which is set out below.

Teaching stories, novels, and plays

Much of what follows can be adapted to the teaching of poetry.

1 First reading in class (only possible with short stories, one-act plays, and poetry). Full-length novels and plays require a combination of selected readings with drama activities. An example of this can be found below, in the section which deals with *Cry, the Beloved Country*. The first reading should be accompanied by an explanation of the more difficult vocabulary (for example, slang, colloquialisms, and idioms) as well as comprehension questions which should be extensive, focusing on the broad outline of the plot, rather than intensive.

2 A discussion on the moral dilemma of the central character in the text. Here the teacher invites the class to 'step into role' as a team of experts trying to resolve the dilemma(s) facing the central characters(s). As 'experts' they could be psychiatrists, marriage guidance counsellors, village elders, or Samaritans, depending on the type of problem they are dealing with.

3 A study of the background archive materials previously prepared by the teacher. Archives can vary greatly in detail, depending on the work being studied. For example, my archives for *Over the Wall* and *Cry, the Beloved Country* were quite detailed, consisting of newspaper articles, maps, pictures, letters and legal documents, while the archive materials I used to stimulate interest in Edgar Allen Poe's *The Fall of the House of Usher* consisted only of a letter supposedly written by Roderick Usher to the narrator of the story, and a picture of a haunted Victorian mansion, which I cut out of a magazine. The archive materials should be placed on a few desks or tables, and the students should carefully study these materials, using dictionaries and encyclopedias to aid their understanding. As far as possible, they should work independently of the teacher. In my presentation of *Over the Wall* they were required to 'step into role' as a team of investigative journalists, and had to report their findings to the class.

4 An analysis of the relationships in the story, using simple cut-out figures which represent the key characters (see Figure 13). Working in groups, the students create 'relationship pictures' by placing the characters in the positions that represent the nature of the characters' relationships with one another. They then explain their picture to the other groups, who can criticize their arrangement.

5 Role play. As a result of stages (3) and (4), the groups now prepare and present interviews with the characters in the story.

6 Wax-work tableaux. In groups the students create waxwork 'pictures' of the key scenes in the story, i.e. they 'freeze' certain scenes while posing as the characters themselves. These tableaux are presented for discussion and criticism to the rest of the class. A few simple 'props' like white sheets, cloaks, shawls, and books are needed for this stage. These tableaux can be photographed and exhibited in sequence with relevant quotations from the text.

7 Dramatization of the key scenes presented in the waxwork tableaux. If there is any dialogue in the scene, the groups can now act out the key scenes.

8 Further detailed text analysis (if necessary).

9 Further discussions on the key issues in the story (if necessary).

10 Writing tasks (if desired).

'Over The Wall'

'Over The Wall' by James Saunders (in *Double Act*, edited by Mark Shackleton, published by Edward Arnold).

Over the Wall is a parable play, in which any number of characters can take part. A narrator tells the story and the islanders act it out. It is about an island with a wall running across it. Who built it, why it was built, or what exists behind it nobody knows or cares – nobody, that is, except one man. He dedicates his entire life to the mystery of the wall, with tragic consequences, and the audience is left to decide whether his devotion to his ideal was heroically tragic or just a comic and stupid obsession.

In this approach, the students will already have read the play, either privately or in class, and the most difficult vocabulary will have been dealt with by the teacher.

It is necessary to build up an archive of materials to provide a realistic background to the play. Such an archive would include:

1 Geographical information: for example a map of the island (I adapted a map of Iceland for this purpose) clearly showing how the wall cuts across the island, together with details about its climate, soil, population, economy, and agriculture. Much of this information is contained in the play, but in some cases it is necessary to improvise details.

2 Historical information: for instance, an old document containing a brief history of the island and the wall, and an account of the first (and last) attempt to cross the wall. All this can be found in the play itself. This can simply be written on faded yellow paper.

3 Current affairs: various newspaper articles showing different accounts of the main plot – 'Madman dies trying to cross Wall'; 'Famous explorer killed crossing treacherous wall'; 'Screaming crowds witness death of stuntman', with pictures or illustrations.

4 Personal details of the central character: e.g. last will and testament; medical reports (by doctor and psychiatrist); death certificate; divorce papers; photographs of family. Much of this can be improvised and typed out with various signatures attached.

Below are some samples of the type of material to be included in the
archive. Other materials needed are a few loose cloaks, some
ordinary sheets, hats, a doctor's white coat and stethoscope, and
some books.

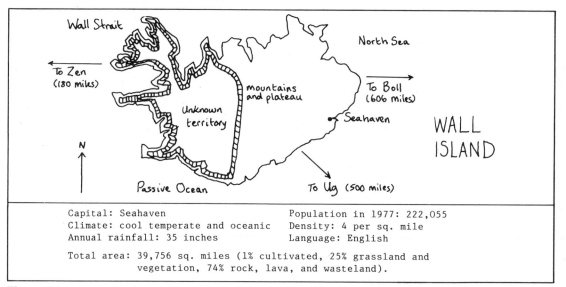

Capital: Seahaven
Climate: cool temperate and oceanic
Annual rainfall: 35 inches

Population in 1977: 222,055
Density: 4 per sq. mile
Language: English

Total area: 39,756 sq. miles (1% cultivated, 25% grassland and
vegetation, 74% rock, lava, and wasteland).

Figure 11

ISLAND ECHO

Madman dies trying to cross Wall

Benjamin Drake, 75-year-old eccentric, died of an
apparent heart-attack yesterday while trying to cross
The Wall, despite warnings from the authorities
that it was unsafe to do so. Police have been unable
to recover his body, as he fell on the forbidden
side of The Wall.

Figure 12

MEDICAL REPORT

Mr Benjamin Drake was a patient of mine for more than
twenty years. During this time, he was repeatedly
warned to give up his obsession with The Wall.
When I saw him last, he was obviously suffering from
stress. In my opinion, he was, at the advanced age
of 75, certainly not fit enough to undertake such
arduous exertion as attempting to cross The Wall.
This could have caused the heart-attack to which he
finally succumbed.

(signed) *A. Wyatt*.....
GENERAL PRACTITIONER

Figure 13

IN CLASS

Stage One

The class is asked to 'step into role' as a team of psychiatrists, to
consider whether the central character in the play was insane or not.
They are also confronted with the choices he was faced with, and
have to decide whether his choices were morally justifiable. The
teacher is the head of the team, and has summoned them all to a
conference to discuss his or her patient, the central character. It is
suggested that the teacher 'steps into role' from the beginning, even
to the extent of wearing a white coat. The choices are written on the
board, as follows:

– As a child, should he have accepted the verdicts on the Wall
  given to him by his parents?

- As a husband, should he have paid more attention to his wife's needs, instead of allowing his obsession with the Wall to destroy his marriage?
- As a father, should he have paid more attention to his children's needs?
- Should the people of the island have tried harder to save him from his obsession?

The objective of this stage is to define the principal moral issue of the play and allow the students to probe the mind of the central character. This stage could last one full session.

Stage Two
Next, the class is asked to 'step into role' as a team of investigative journalists. In groups, they inspect the prepared archive (laid out on various tables), and report back to the class on what they have found out. Each group could tackle a different section of the archive, but the reporting back should be in the sequence of: geographical facts — historical facts — current affairs — personal detail, so that the full background emerges, from the factual to the abstract/personal. The objective of this stage is to give the students a clear, realistic, and digestible background to the play, and to allow them to see the text's universal implications. Students should be urged at all times to remain 'in role' and never to forget the parts they are playing.

Stage Three
Still as journalists, the students now arrange a series of cut-out figures into 'relationship pictures', illustrated in Figure 14. They have to place the cut-outs near to, on top of, far away from, next to, or under each other, to show what they understand about the relationships between the central character and the other people in his life. They should, of course, refer to the text to do this, and they can move about and criticize one another's pictures.

The objective of this stage is to allow the students to look critically at the closeness or distance in the relationships of the central characters in the play. Stages Two and Three could last one session.

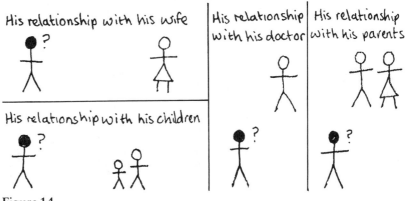

Figure 14

Stage Four

As a result of the journalism sequence, we can now do a number of simulated radio interviews. In groups, the students prepare interviews with:

a. Drake's wife;
b. his doctor;
c. one of his acquaintances;
d. his children;
e. some of the spectators who witnessed his death.

The interviews could be tape-recorded, or you could make a video. The interviews must be based, as far as possible, on the text itself, but some improvisation may be called for. All the interviews take place after the death of the central character.

The objective of this stage is to extend the simple 'placing' activity of Stage 3. It allows characters other than the central character to step out of the text, and to assume reality in the eyes of the learners. The preparation of the interviews will also show how well the students understand the human relationships in the play. It will also throw some light on the motives of the central character, as viewed by those who knew him well. This stage could last one session.

Stage Five

Now the students are told that they are going to visit a wax museum. At the museum, they will see the story of *Over the Wall* presented as a series of waxwork tableaux. They themselves are the creators of these waxwork pictures. In groups, they work on creating waxwork pictures based on the key scenes from the play. They are to pose as the characters, and should use the props provided by the teacher to create their scene.

Students can walk around the classroom, commenting critically on the waxwork pictures of the other groups. In all of these activities, the teacher has a background role, helping and advising only when asked by the students. And throughout the various stages, the students have to consult the text, and interpret it as best as they can, thereby achieving what the teacher ultimately wants them to do: to read and understand the text.

The objective of this stage is the creation of a static picture of the plot, the first stage in the eventual dramatization of the play. It deals principally with the main plot, and serves to bind all the different strands together.

Stage Six

Bringing the static waxworks to life. The groups who have prepared the various scenes as waxwork tableaux now do a dramatized playreading of their scene, working on each scene in sequence. This is an enjoyable way of rounding off the work done. The teacher and class might even at this stage decide to perform the play, which would further serve to reinforce their understanding and appreciation of it.

After the above six stages, some work can be done on text analysis, with discussion sessions on the obsessions of famous characters in history, for example Scott of the Antarctic, Napoleon, and Joan of Arc. With the understanding gained through the use of drama, these sessions will be richer and easier to assimilate.

'Cry, the Beloved Country'

SOURCE

Cry, the Beloved Country by Alan Paton, published by Jonathan Cape.

In teaching this book to an upper-intermediate class, I combined selected class-readings with the same techniques used to teach *Over the Wall*. The rest of the reading was done privately by the students.

PREPARATION

To stimulate interest in the book, I started the students off with a debate on capital punishment. Then I gave each group a copy of Absalom Kumalo's final letter from the condemned cell in Pretoria Central Prison, and asked them to determine as much as they could about his background, his crime, and his family. Once I had got them interested in the human dilemma of the story, I introduced the social and political background of South Africa, once again using the archive method outlined above. It was a time of great political upheaval and unrest in South Africa, so the class was exposed daily to the realities of the situation encountered in the book through news broadcasts and TV programmes, which further stimulated their interest in the book.

IN CLASS

The class presented the key scenes of the book both as waxwork tableaux and as dramatized playreadings, and also produced essays on the various characters they met in the book. Several colleagues helped me to produce the necessary archive materials, as I needed different sets of handwriting to copy out the many letters in the book, in order to give them the necessary impression of authenticity.

Separate discussion sessions were also held on the role and influence of the murdered Arthur Jarvis, and the influence of gold-mining on the Southern African community. Finally, we dealt with Paton's use of English in the novel, with its rich infusion of Zulu and other African words and idioms.

Teaching poetry through drama
– some suggestions

1 Choose a number of poems around a central theme (for example the seasons, work, war, relationships, childhood). Each group selects, or is given, one poem to prepare as a choral reading. They have to decide on the most suitable presentation of the reading: the number of solo parts, the arrangement of male and female voices, changes in pace and volume, etc. Set a time-limit on their preparation. When they are ready, they should read their poem to the class. The class can now offer constructive criticism of their interpretation, and it should be possible for them to improve on a second reading.

2 Choose a narrative poem. After reading and discussion, let the students dramatize the story in groups. Here are some examples that can be used for this purpose:

'Frankie and Johnny' (traditional American)
'Telephone Conversation' (Wole Soyinkwa)
'Interruption at the Opera House' (Brian Patten)
'A Case of Murder' (Vernon Scannell)
'Victor. A Ballad' (W.H. Auden)

Note: Instead of acting out the story in words, the group can present it as a mime, while one or more members of the same group read out the poem.

3 Poems rich in onomatopoeic words, for example 'The Listeners', lend themselves particularly well to dramatization. The class can build up a 'sound picture' of the poem, by imitating the various sounds in the poem. They can also be asked to listen to the first reading of the poem (by you) with their eyes shut, and they can then discuss what they heard or what images formed in their minds while they were listening to the poem. More adventurous classes can also interpret the poem through movement and dance–drama. Some examples of suitable poems are:

'Anthem for Doomed Youth' (Wilfred Owen)
'Jazz Fantasia' (Carl Sandburg)
'The Preludes (I)' (T.S.Eliot)
'Crusader' (Roger McGough)

4 Cut out a number of pictures that could represent a non-narrative poem. In groups or pairs, the students discuss which picture best captures the feeling of the poem. Alternatively, they could try to draw a picture to represent the poem themselves.

5 Get the class to prepare (in groups or pairs) imaginary interviews with the poet on the subject of the poem, or with the characters in the poem.

6 Ask the class to imagine the background/context of a particular poem (see 'The Listeners').

7 Silent reading, followed by an interpretation of the mood of the poem, e.g. light-hearted, cynical, solemn, bitter, etc. Groups then try to capture this mood in their reading of the poem.

8 Present the class with the first part of a narrative poem. Ask them to improvise continuations (this can be attempted either in verse or prose). They can then compare their improvisations with the original poem.

'The Listeners'

<table>
<tr>
<td>SOURCE</td>
<td>Collected Poems of Walter de la Mare, published by Faber and Faber (also available in many anthologies).</td>
</tr>
<tr>
<td>IN CLASS</td>
<td>

Stage One

This particular poem by Walter de la Mare is rich in onomatopoeic elements, so the initial reading and discussion was followed by the students building up a 'sound picture' of the poem, in the order in which the sounds occur in the poem. The aim of the 'sound picture' was to help them to imagine what the ghostly listeners in the house could actually hear, from the moment when the rider approaches in the distance until he leaves. The sequence was written on the board, and the students then suggested ways of imitating the sounds. The sequence developed as follows:

a. The sound of the approaching horse – imitated by the class drumming on their desks with their fingers: first one student, then a few, and finally everyone.
b. The whinny of the horse as it is reined in – performed by one student.
c. The jingle of the stirrups and spurs – achieved by jingling a bunch of keys.
d. Footsteps – 'walking' bunched fists over a desk (done by one student).
e. The first knock – done on the desk.
f. 'Is there anybody there?' – spoken hesitantly by one reader.
g. The horse moving and eating the grass – a champing sound, accompanied by the jingle of the keys.
h. The sound of a bird flying – achieved by flapping the pages of a book.
i. The second, louder knock.
j. The voice again, louder this time.
k. The hooting of owls (done by a group of girls) to emphasize the silence that greets him.
l. The movement of the horse again.
m. The loudest knock of all.
n. The voice (almost a shout).
o. The hooting of owls again.
p. Footsteps going away.
q. The jingle of the stirrups.

</td>
</tr>
</table>

r. The sound of the horse's hooves on the stone path (achieved by knocking the keys against a hard-backed file).

s. The sound of the horse galloping, gradually dying away in the distance (the entire class drummed their fingers on their desks at first, and then, at a signal from the teacher, gradually stopped until only one student was left, who continued for another ten seconds).

Not only did this create the actual atmosphere of the poem, but the students were also left with a heightened understanding of the contents and vocabulary. This stage achieved all the key notions listed in the introduction to this chapter, especially the slowing down of experience and the infusion of dramatic tension.

Stage Two

The second stage involved a choral reading of the poem, organized as follows, and 'conducted' by the teacher:

TEXT

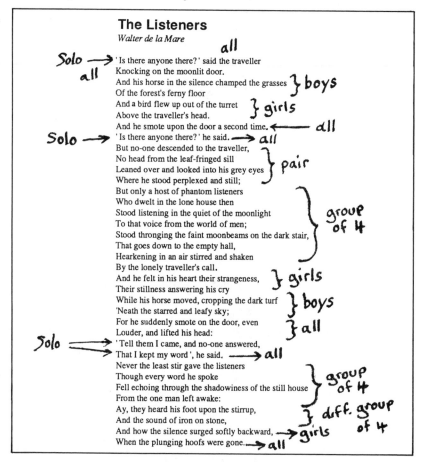

The Listeners
Walter de la Mare

> all
> *Solo* → 'Is there anyone there?' said the traveller
> all
> Knocking on the moonlit door.
> And his horse in the silence champed the grasses } boys
> Of the forest's ferny floor
> And a bird flew up out of the turret } girls
> Above the traveller's head.
> And he smote upon the door a second time. ← all
> *Solo* → 'Is there anyone there?' he said. → all
> But no-one descended to the traveller,
> No head from the leaf-fringed sill
> Leaned over and looked into his grey eyes } pair
> Where he stood perplexed and still;
> But only a host of phantom listeners
> Who dwelt in the lone house then
> Stood listening in the quiet of the moonlight } group of 4
> To that voice from the world of men;
> Stood thronging the faint moonbeams on the dark stair,
> That goes down to the empty hall,
> Hearkening in an air stirred and shaken
> By the lonely traveller's call.
> And he felt in his heart their strangeness, } girls
> Their stillness answering his cry
> While his horse moved, cropping the dark turf } boys
> 'Neath the starred and leafy sky;
> For he suddenly smote on the door, even } all
> Louder, and lifted his head:
> *Solo* → 'Tell them I came, and no-one answered,
> That I kept my word', he said. → all
> Never the least stir gave the listeners
> Though every word he spoke } group of 4
> Fell echoing through the shadowiness of the still house
> From the one man left awake:
> Ay, they heard his foot upon the stirrup, } diff. group of 4
> And the sound of iron on stone,
> And how the silence surged softly backward, → girls
> When the plunging hoofs were gone. → all

The aim of this stage was to teach the students the correct stress, intonation, and rhythm of the poem, and also to sort out any pronunciation difficulties. The blend of solo and group voices, of the lighter girls' voices and deeper boys' voices produced a very effective choral interpretation of the poem. They were invited to 'step into role' and to read with the correct emotional intensity:

the solo reader's initial nervousness developing into a shout of anguish, and the group reading about the 'host of phantom listeners' injecting an eerie and ethereal note into their reading.

Stage Three
The third stage involved group discussions on the story behind the poem. This included straightforward comprehension questions, as well as speculation about the identities of the speaker and the listeners – what their relationships could have been, what promise he had made and why, the reason for his absence, why the house is deserted, etc. This was to encourage the students to 'see beyond' the printed words, and also to encourage empathy with the main character. The session was concluded with another choral reading of the poem. For homework, they were asked to write the story of the poem.

This is just one of a series of techniques designed to help learners to interpret poetry. Dorothy Heathcote herself uses many of the ideas outlined in this chapter, for example the waxwork tableaux and the relationship pictures, to teach longer narrative poems such as Keats's 'The Eve of St Agnes'.

Teaching simplified literature

At elementary and pre-intermediate levels, the teacher needs to rely on simplified literature to help learners with their reading. Apart from individual study with a range of graded readers, some of the simplified works can be exploited to good effect in class. Here are a few suggestions.

1 Dramatized reading: This can be done in a variety of ways – either by the teacher with a good student reader, or by selected students, or by the whole class, reading in chorus.

2 Improvisation before and after reading the story. See the example of 'The Ticket Inspector' (below) for an improvisation that precedes the reading. This elicits the students' existing language before teaching the new language of the text. After reading, the students can improvise continuations to the stories, prompted by suggestions from the teacher. Alternatively, they can try to improvise the whole story, aided only by some cues written on the board.

3 Reading accompanied by mime: This is especially useful when the story contains plenty of action.

4 Some of the suggestions for poetry can also be applied here, especially building up a 'sound picture', choosing or drawing pictures to represent the text, and improvising continuations of incomplete stories. Piers Plowright's *Read English* contains stories written in dramatic episodes, employing mainly direct speech. With each episode the tension increases, but the ending is left open for students to speculate about the conclusion of the story. Two methods that work well with *Read English* are:

a. using the Total Physical Response approach: the teacher reads the story slowly, while selected students perform the actions (or mime them when realistic actions are not possible);
b. using dramatized playreading: selected students read and act out the dialogues.

The book is accompanied by an excellent cassette recording, which I used for 'copy reading' to teach intonation and pronunciation.

Finally, there are the excellent *Off-Stage!* and *Further Off-Stage!* by Doug Case and Ken Wilson, which contain a variety of comic sketches for reading and performance. Here is how I have approached one of their sketches with a group of elementary students.

'The Ticket Inspector'

SOURCE

Off-Stage! Sketches from the English Teaching Theatre by Doug Case and Ken Wilson, published by Heinemann Educational Books, 1979

IN CLASS

Stage One
The class is shown the photograph of the passenger and the ticket inspector that accompanies the text, and asked to describe what they see.

Stage Two

Now the teacher introduces the story as follows:

A man went to the station. He wanted to visit a friend in the next town, and needed to take the train. He didn't have any money, so he simply got on to the train without buying a ticket. He sat down in a comfortable first-class compartment, and began to read his newspaper. The train started moving out of the station. It began to travel faster and faster. *Suddenly, the door of the man's compartment was flung open . . .*

Stage Three
Now the class takes up the story. The teacher guides the story with these questions:

– Who do you think opened the door?
– What did he say?
– What did the man reply?
– Why did he say that?
– What did the inspector say next?
– What did the man reply?
– How did the inspector begin to feel?

– How did the man feel?
– How would *you* feel if you were the man or the inspector?
– What did the man finally say?
– What was the inspector's reply?
– What did the man say then?
– Was the inspector amused, angry, or bored?
– Did the inspector throw the man off the train? Why/Why not?
– How did the story end?

Stage Four
As the class responds to the questions, the teacher builds up the
dialogue on the board, or on the overhead projector, correcting any
mistakes as they arise.

Stage Five
Now use two students to act out the newly-created sketch. Simple
classroom props will do – a chair, a newspaper, a little note-pad for
the inspector, and perhaps a cap for him as well. With a bright class,
write down only some of the cues on the board. The actors can then
use these cues to create the dialogue. However, with a weak class,
simply write out the whole dialogue and allow them to use it. Insist
on a proper imitation of reality, e.g. moving with the motion of the
train, expressing emotions such as anger, irritation,
embarrassment, fear, etc.

Stage Six
Now hand out copies of the sketch, and do silent reading.

TEXT   **Scene**   A compartment on a train

Characters A passenger on a train
A ticket inspector
A steward and a waiter
*The passenger is sitting in a compartment on a train. He is
reading a newspaper. The steward opens the door.*

Steward Coffee!
Passenger No, thanks.
*The passenger closes the door, and continues reading. The waiter opens
the door.*
Waiter Seats for dinner!
Passenger No, thanks.
*The passenger closes the door again, and continues reading. The ticket
inspector opens the door.*
Inspector Tickets!
Passenger No, thanks.
Inspector Pardon?
Passenger I don't want a ticket, thank you.
Inspector I'm not *selling* tickets, sir.
Passenger No?
Inspector No. I want to see *your* ticket.

Passenger Oh, I haven't got a ticket.

Inspector You haven't got a ticket?

Passenger No. I never buy a ticket.

Inspector Why not?

Passenger Well, they *are very* expensive, you know.

Inspector Sir, you're travelling on a train. When people travel on a train, they always buy a ticket.

Passenger Er . . .

Inspector And *this* is a first-class compartment.

Passenger Yes, it *is* very nice, isn't it?

Inspector No, sir. I mean: this is a *first-class* compartment. When people travel in a first-class compartment, they always buy a first-class ticket.

They look at each other for a moment.

Passenger No, they don't.

Inspector What?

Passenger A lot of people don't buy tickets. The Queen doesn't buy a ticket, does she? Eh? Eh?

Inspector No, sir, but *she's* a famous person.

Passenger And what about you? Where's yours?

Inspector Mine?

Passenger Yes, yours. Your ticket. Have *you* got a ticket?

Inspector Me, sir?

Passenger Yes, you.

Inspector No, I haven't got a ticket.

Passenger Ooh – are you a famous person?

Inspector (*Flattered*) Famous? Well, not very – (*Back to normal*). Sir, I am a ticket inspector. I inspect tickets. Are you going to show me your ticket?

Passenger No, I haven't got a ticket.

Inspector I see.

The ticket inspector puts his hand into his pocket.

Passenger What are you doing to do?

Inspector I'm going to write your name in my book.

Passenger Oh.

Inspector What is your name, sir?

Passenger Mickey Mouse.

The inspector begins to write.

Inspector Mickey –

Passenger – Mouse. M–O–U–S–E.

The inspector stops writing.

Inspector Your *name*, sir?

Passenger Karl Marx? William Shakespeare? Charles Dickens?

Inspector I see, sir. Well, if you're not going to tell me your name, please leave the train.

Passenger Pardon?
Inspector Leave the train.
Passenger I can't.
Inspector You can't what?
Passenger I can't leave the train.
Inspector Why not?
Passenger It's moving.
Inspector Not *now*, sir. At the next station.
Passenger Oh.
Inspector It's in the book, sir. When you travel by train, you buy a
  ticket, and if you don't buy a ticket, you –
Passenger ⎫
Inspector ⎬ – leave the train.
Inspector Here we are, sir. We're coming to a station. Please leave
  the train now.
Passenger Now?
Inspector Yes, sir. I'm sorry, but –
Passenger Oh, that's OK.
Inspector – it's in the book, and – What did you say?
Passenger I said: 'That's OK'.
Inspector OK?
Passenger Yes, this is my station. Goodbye.
  The passenger leaves the train.

Stage Seven
Do a dramatized playreading with selected students. The rest of the
class can comment critically on aspects of interpretation and
performance. This can be followed by a second group's
dramatization.

Stage Eight
Finally, listen to a recording of 'The Ticket Inspector' on the *Off-
Stage!* cassette, and comment briefly on pronunciation and
intonation.

By preceding the actual reading of the sketch with the students'
own improvised version, I was able to tap their existing language
and lay the foundation for a fuller understanding of the script.
Needless to say, the students found the improvisation more
challenging and exciting than the playreading itself, since it
consisted of their own suggestions. Some of the performers insisted
on improvising even further during the enactment, and their
versions frequently proved highly original and inventive.

References and recommended reading

Benton, Michael and **Peter** (eds). 1971. *Touchstones*. London: Hodder and Stoughton.

Brendon, P. and **W. Shaw** (eds). 1967. *Readings They've Liked*. London: Macmillan.

Case, Doug and **Ken Wilson**. 1978. *Off-Stage!*. London: Heinemann.

Gibson, James (ed). 1975. *Let the Poet Choose*. London: Harrap.

Paton, Alan. 1948. *Cry, the Beloved Country*. London: Jonathan Cape.

Plowright, Piers. 1973. *Read English*. London: Heinemann.

Shackleton, Mark. 1985. *Double Act* (for 'Over the Wall'). London: Edward Arnold.

Summerfield, Geoffrey (ed). 1968. *Voices (the Third Book)*. London: Penguin.

Wagner, Betty Jane. 1976. *Dorothy Heathcote – Drama as a Learning Medium*. London: Hutchinson.

Section Two
The drama project

7 The place of the drama project in language teaching

Introduction

Why is it worth while working on a drama project if you use drama in your classroom teaching already? What special merits does a project have, and how can it benefit your students' everyday progress? To answer these questions, let us consider some responses from students who have been involved in various drama projects which culminated in a full stage production.

It's fun. (Eva; German, intermediate level)
I'm actually using the words of the play in my daily conversation.
    (Manuel; Spanish, upper-intermediate)
I feel in control of my English. (Regina; Polish, elementary)
We're all friends, and I have much conversation in English. (Khalid;
    Kuwaiti, intermediate)
I learned more English from the play than in class. (Ernst; Swiss,
    upper-intermediate)
When's the next play? (Ken; Japanese, pre-intermediate)

These students all took part in six-week drama projects at the Institute for Applied Language Studies, University of Edinburgh (IALS). Their spontaneous responses illustrate why the project is such a satisfactory and rewarding way of teaching and learning English (or any other language, for that matter). In this chapter we shall examine the theoretical and practical considerations underlying the drama project, prompted by the students' own quoted responses.

'It's fun' (Eva)

The most basic reward of drama is that it is enjoyable to do. First of all, there is usually a lot of tension-relieving laughter, as students warm up physically through games, exercises, breathing techniques, vocal warm-ups, mime, and improvisation. There is a lot of touching and other physical contact during these sessions as well, which further breaks down barriers and inhibitions, and helps to shape a happy and co-operative group.

Secondly, the learning environment is altered or changed completely. Rehearsals take place either in a drama studio or (more commonly) in a large classroom in which the desks have been pushed away to create ample space for movement and running about.

Thirdly, each session brings the reward of being allowed to 'speak out', express emotions, and 'take centre stage' as each student realizes that his or her contribution, no matter how small, is of vital importance to the project. Even the most inhibited person enjoys being the centre of attention at least once, and the project ensures that (to paraphrase Andy Warhol) 'everyone will be a star for five minutes'.

Eva was a tense, unhappy girl until the play *The Dear Departed* allowed her to express a great deal of the considerable passion and anger suppressed inside her. She proved to be quite a gifted comic actor.

'I'm actually using the words of the play in my daily conversation.' (Manuel)

It is the dream of every teacher that 'what goes in will eventually come out'. We all hope that our students will assimilate the language we teach, and start to use it naturally. A drama project can guarantee that within six weeks those involved will be able to use the words of the play not only during rehearsals, but spontaneously at other times as well, provided that the language of the play meets the students' linguistic needs and is accessible to them; and provided that the lines are learned through rehearsals and not through 'parrot-fashion' memorization.

Rehearsals usually concentrate intensively on small, coherent passages from the play. The lines are thus assimilated through constant repetition, which is assisted by the use of gesture, facial expressions, movement, emotions, and background knowledge, and the assimilation is reinforced regularly by other rehearsals.

Manuel's remarks are particularly pertinent to his own situation. As a doctor, he was the obvious choice for the role of Dr Ginsberg in Agatha Christie's *The Patient*. The play taught him both medical and conversational English, and as he was rather soft-spoken, it also helped him to project loudly and clearly. And by the end, he felt far more confident about the prospect of coping with British patients.

So instead of learning functions and notions in English in isolation or separate units (a principle of so many so-called 'communicative' textbooks), participants in a play are able to acquire a considerable amount of language naturally in a fully contextualized and integrated manner.

I usually test the above assertion during the fourth week of the project. Students have to run through the play without the aid of the script, and without stopping or hesitating too long. In other words, they have to try to get through the play by improvisation and ad-libbing. They usually manage to produce close approximations of their lines. Once they realize that they are capable of improvising effectively, a lot of their anxiety about learning their lines disappears, and consequently they feel more confident and are even able to memorize their lines better. And surely the most difficult thing to do in a foreign language is ad-libbing under stress! This experience gives students renewed pride and confidence in their ability to use the language, which helps to increase their motivation and loyalty towards the project.

'I feel in control of my English.' (Regina)

This response came from a Polish student who, with only four weeks of English to her credit, took on quite a demanding role in *The Patient*, the role of Brenda, the secretary of Bryan Wingfield. At the end of the project, she was promoted from the elementary class to the intermediate one, confident and highly motivated.

She had learnt that she could control the language and that it was not a terrifying, alien system, but a medium for communicating the same feelings, attitudes, and sentiments as she expressed in her mother tongue, Polish. Through the weeks of the project, she had learnt to express fear, hatred, anger, love, and suspicion (among other feelings) in English, and during the performances it was clear to her that the audience understood, reacted to, and appreciated her performance in English.

In Regina, the almost automatic resistance that we all put up against the unknown had been broken down by the project, and her confidence in her own abilities to achieve success was further enhanced. But she contributed a great deal towards that too, by being such a lively, extrovert, and hard-working participant.

'We're all friends, and I have much conversational English.' (Khalid)

A drama project is a valuable means of improving interpersonal communication. As a group working towards a common goal, students tend to make friends very easily within the relaxed atmosphere of rehearsals. They tend to socialize together more, and some long-lasting friendships are forged. It is impossible to remain isolated if you take part in such a project, and equally impossible not to feel relaxed and at ease with others whom you have seen rolling about on the floor, pulling faces, in a passionate embrace with someone else, or doing any of those weird and wonderful things that drama permits.

Naturally, a lot of conversation takes place during a rehearsal, and it is through this spontaneous interaction that a great deal of language is acquired. The learning of the lines is a formal, conscious activity, while the acquisition of language through the discussions during rehearsals is an informal, unconscious activity.

This corresponds, as I pointed out in the introduction to this book, to Krashen's theory of learning and acquisition.

Here are some of the topics that will be covered, through informal conversation, during a rehearsal:

- How to approach a particular scene.
- How the lines should be said.
- Commentary on individual performances.
- Scene shifting, lights, and sound effects.
- Clothing and make-up.
- Movements and gestures.
- Problem areas.
- Feelings about the play and the characters in it.
- How to publicize the production.
- Socializing after rehearsals – where to meet for drinks, and the obligatory celebratory dinner after the show.
- Personal difficulties.

We can see from the above that the teacher in charge of a drama project does not have to search endlessly for something to stimulate conversation. The play, and the students' responses to it, will provide all the stimulus that is needed. Khalid, another medical doctor, found it difficult to socialize outside the class, owing to his family commitments, and consequently could not get enough informal conversation practice. But the project provided him with as much as he needed, as well as eight new friends.

'I learned more English from the play than in class.' (Ernst)

Some learners instinctively rebel against conventional styles of teaching. They are the *blasé* students who come to class prepared to be bored, and will, if the opportunity presents itself, disrupt the teacher's well-laid plans for the lesson. Only the unusual or the unconventional will shock them out of their torpor.

The project turned out to be the only thing Ernst looked forward to. Apart from his casual attitudes to classwork, he was also in the unfortunate position of being too advanced for the rest of his (upper-intermediate) class. The play, in which he had a starring role (that of a Sherlock Holmes kind of sleuth), proved to be the only thing that stretched him intellectually and linguistically.

'When's the next play?' (Ken)

Despite Richard Via's assertion (one I endorse fully) that '*everyone can act*' (Via 1972), there are still some students who regard drama projects with suspicion and refuse to 'make fools of themselves'. Ken was a student who consistently refused to be drawn into any of the projects. But, after attending a successful performance of *Us and Them*, performed by his fellow-students, he suddenly became very eager to participate in the next project. He had been stimulated by the success of the production, the obvious delight and enjoyment of his peers, and the great strides they had made with their English. He subsequently took part in *Over the Wall* most successfully and happily.

Conclusions

From the foregoing we can draw several conclusions. A drama project is an enjoyable, informal means of learning a language – so it is a valuable supplement to classroom learning. It helps the learner acquire new vocabulary and structures in a fully contextualized and integrated manner – so it fulfils the aims of the communicative approach. By making the language more accessible to the learner, it builds confidence in the learner's ability to learn the language.

A drama project takes full cognizance of the socio-psychological aspects of learning – so it involves the whole person, evoking the total human response. For some students it can be an alternative means of learning the language, and for them it can produce a far more positive response than normal classroom teaching.

By stimulating awareness in the learner of the underlying processes involved in learning a language, the drama project can help learners to extend their range of learning 'tools'. And finally, the drama project can build appreciation and understanding of the culture and codes of behaviour of the target language – so it can reduce resistance in the learner towards that language.

Acknowledgement
My thanks and sincere appreciation to the students who have allowed me to quote them in this chapter: Eva Brachmueller, Manuel Giner, Regina van Bennekum, Khalid Al Shalawi, Ernst Lueber, and Kenichiro Miki.

8 General criteria for setting up a drama project

A drama project with language learning and acquisition as its main focus frees you, as teacher–producer, from many of the demands and constraints of conventional theatre productions. You can, for example, dispense with elaborate stage properties and light and sound effects, and concentrate instead on the language itself. With careful planning and preparation, any language teacher should be able to put on a successful production. This chapter looks at precisely what is involved in the planning of and preparation for a drama project. The starting point, of course, is the play itself.

The play

Plays for language-learning projects should ideally fulfil all of the following conditions:

1 They should be written in contemporary English. Generally, this means plays dating from the 1950s to the present day, although some one-act plays written in the 1930s and 1940s are also suitable.

2 They should contain plenty of conversational interaction: it is best to avoid plays with long monologues. Apart from the fact that such long monologues are contrary to the aim of the project, which seeks to involve all the members of the group most of the time, they place a lot of strain on the student who has to speak them, and could encourage parrot-fashion memorization.

3 It is important to have as many parts as possible (no fewer than six), with each part being large enough to justify the language-learning aims of the project.

4 The main plot should be fairly simple.

5 The theme must be interesting or amusing, but you should avoid topics which are too culture-specific: the play must not give offence to the students, and it should be possible for them to identify with the characters in the play as well as with the situation.

6 The contents should be relatively concrete. Genres like melodrama, symbolic drama, or the theatre of the absurd generally work well only with very advanced students. Genres like crime and detection, romance, domestic dramas, parable plays, and comedy all work very well with groups of mixed levels and abilities.

7 It should be either a one-act play or a very short full-length one.

8 It should fit a rehearsal period of not more than six weeks, to avoid laziness or boredom setting in. Students should be given the approximate date of performance at the beginning, so that they know that they are working towards a specific end.

9 If you can, you should choose plays written specifically for native speakers, but which are still linguistically accessible to the learners (hence the avoidance of the more abstract genres). Simplified plays written with language learners in mind are useful for classroom drama, but not for project work.

The following plays can be used successfully with groups of mixed levels and abilities:

The Patient (Agatha Christie)
The Dear Departed (Stanley Houghton)
The Rising Generation (Ann Jellico)
The Man Who Wouldn't Go To Heaven (F. Sladen-Smith)
Arthur (David Cregan)
Ernie's Incredible Illucinations (Alan Ayckbourn)
Over the Wall (James Saunders)
Us and Them (David Campton)

Details of these plays, and of several useful anthologies, will be found in the Bibliography at the end of this book.

The people

The participants should ideally be volunteers at the post-elementary to advanced levels. All the students who turn up for the first meeting should be accommodated, either as actors, understudies, or stage managers, though it should be added that one rarely has an overwhelming response if the project is done on a voluntary basis. Gradually the less committed students will drop out, until only a core group remains. All of these should be given a part to play.

A special level of interest and commitment is required of the teacher, since this type of project is not a mainstream language syllabus activity; it is time-intensive and demands organizational skills. But you do not need to have had acting experience, or any other type of theatrical experience (although naturally it would be a great advantage).

Time

Currently, EFL course directors and planners are paying a good deal of attention to all kinds of project work on cultural, historical, socio-political, and literary themes. A drama project, which can involve some or all of these elements, also has the advantage of being presented to an audience at the end. It should be entirely feasible to include it as part of the students' formal programme of study, which is already the happy situation in some centres. If this is the case, two sessions or periods per week should provide ample time for the development of the project, with extra sessions in out-of-class hours shortly before the play is staged. If the project is an integral part of the students' course, it would also be feasible to extend the minimum period of six weeks' preparation to eight or even ten weeks.

While such a situation is the ideal, most teachers will still be obliged to conduct the project on a voluntary, extra-mural basis, in out-of-class hours. In this case, it is much better to plan a tight schedule within the limit of six weeks – a period short enough to sustain interest and motivation, but sufficient to cover the average one-act play of 15–20 pages.

The number of rehearsal sessions per week will naturally depend on your own schedule and the willingness of the students, but two sessions each week, of an average length of ninety minutes each, should be your absolute minimum. In addition, the final two Saturdays before opening night should be included in your rehearsal schedule. This type of arrangement carries the benefit of a 'quick return' for the student volunteers, and can also accommodate those students attending short-term courses.

Space

For projects intended for groups ranging in number from 8 to 15 students, you will need the largest room available. If the centre has its own theatre or drama studio you are indeed fortunate, although working in an ordinary classroom where the desks or tables have simply been pushed out of the way also has its advantages. The classroom is less intimidating and has fewer distractions than the

An ordinary classroom transformed into a stage

theatre, and it is easier to focus on language learning in this more familiar environment. And it requires very little to change the classroom into a theatre – a few screens, a couple of white sheets, a tape-recorder with sound effects, and appropriate, if basic, outfits for the student actors are all you need.

Group dynamics

Good group dynamics, which enable classes to cohere and co-operate smoothly, don't just happen, as any astute teacher will know. From the very beginning of the project, every single game that is played, every physical exercise or vocal warm-up, should be geared towards generating good group dynamics. The teacher's own warm, friendly, and relaxed presence is a vital factor in creating the right atmosphere. In a project of this nature, it is important that every student has a part to play. No one should be fobbed off with the promise of backstage work or being someone's understudy – this will simply drive them away. Backstage work can always be done by the group itself, or by other teachers. And should there be any emergency, for example sudden illness, a teacher could always be drafted in to read the part.

Games to generate good group dynamics

One problem that can wreak havoc with a production is that of 'drifters' – students who are assigned roles, attend the first few rehearsals, and then just drop out for a multitude of reasons. An unexpected wedding in Saudi Arabia cost me one of my principal actors in *Over the Wall*, while mounting anxiety over an examination robbed me of my excellent Syrian doctor in *Us and Them*.

It is therefore very important to have a clear schedule prepared, and to tell anyone who cannot adhere strictly to this schedule that it might be better if they dropped out of the group unless they can sustain the level of commitment required. It is also crucial to get to know each student actor well, in order to sort out any problems that may arise, and to know who your most loyal and trustworthy stalwarts are.

Encouraging weaker students

You will have to make allowance for the fact that some individuals may need more attention than others.Give such students extra help outside normal rehearsal time, so as not to waste anyone's time. You could meet with these students once a week, to help them with the correct interpretation of their lines, and particularly with the pronunciation. Your own model in this case will be crucial. If you have a very busy schedule, you might wish to enlist the assistance of other teachers to help you with these problem cases. However, there is a danger that their interpretation of the lines may differ sharply from what you want it to be, unless they have worked on the project from the beginning.

When all else fails, you should record on to a cassette all the lines to be spoken by a student having difficulties. Leave gaps so that he or she can record the lines as well, and then compare his or her own reading with that of the teacher. The student can then take the cassette home for individual study and memorization.

Sometimes it is also a good idea to have paired practice during a rehearsal, pairing off the better and more advanced students with the weaker ones. Students are generally sympathetic to the weaker members of the group (particularly if the group dynamics are sound), and do not regard this as a waste of time.

Help from other teachers

I like to use other teachers in my drama projects, not only as an emergency measure when a student falls ill, but also as principal actors and stage managers.This has greatly aided the smooth operation of the project. The presence of other teachers helps to relax the students, because they can learn a great deal from watching a native speaker perform, and they feel more secure with a teacher on stage with them. Such a teacher is also an effective on-stage prompt.

Frequently, both the teacher-director and another teacher will form part of the cast, thus ensuring a more accurate interpretation of the play and soothing any possible stage nerves. The most important thing to remember when using other teachers is that you are the director. You should be open to all suggestions, but the students should not be confused by any doubt about who is the leader of the project.

Discipline

In her book on the work of Dorothy Heathcote, Betty Jane Wagner writes:

> Classroom drama uses the elements of the art of the theatre. Like any art, it is highly disciplined, not free. Like painters, sculptors, or dancers, the participants are held taut in the discipline of an art form. Thus there are rules of the craft that must be followed if the implicit is to be made explicit, if the classroom drama is going to work so that, as in theatre, a slice of life can be taken up and examined.

As the students involved in a drama project will be kept actively involved throughout a rehearsal, you will rarely encounter the kind of disciplinary problems that sometimes crop up in class. On two issues, however, you will need to be very firm:

1 lateness: stress that time is limited, and that each delay could affect the production adversely;

2 excessive facetiousness and tomfoolery: if a hectic warm-up does not help to curb this, allow the students ten minutes of it and then insist on more concentration. Use expressions like 'Concentrate!', 'Remain in role!', and 'Right, action!'

Serious disciplinary problems should be dealt with on an individual basis.It would never do to humiliate a student in front of his or her peers, not when you are expecting the students to give their best to the project.

At all times, remain enthusiastic, cheerful but firm. Start rehearsals on time, even if everyone required is not present. Show them that you believe in, and are fully committed to, the success of the project. Eventually, your own confidence will rub off on them.

The first session

Your first meeting with the group should contain all the essential ingredients of future rehearsals. It should also be fun, and hold the promise of future enjoyment. Start off with physical warm-ups, such as the exercise routine outlined in Chapter 4. Follow this with the breathing exercises from the same chapter. Add two vocal warm-ups, like

> the tip of the tongue, the teeth and the lips
> hot coffee in a proper, copper coffee-pot

and end on a shout: 'TOPEKA!'

Now play the following group ensemble games, to help the students to get to know each other. All these games can be found in Chapter 2.

> Handshakes
> My name's X, and what about you?
> Not me!
> Cup ball
> Simon says
> Ear to ear
> Every picture tells a story.

You may not have time for all of these, in which case you should use just the first four games.

If it is possible, you should pre-record a group of teachers reading the play. Give out copies of the play to the students. Explain the plot to them, and list the characters. Be careful not to give too much detail, however. Now let them listen to the recording while following the play on their scripts.

You should have formed some idea of individual students' voice quality and ability during the games. On the basis of this, select certain students to do the first reading of the play. Then answer any questions they may have at this stage. Next, hand out copies of the rehearsal schedule, and go through it with them, pointing out the dates of performances.

Now you can either ask students which part they would like to play, or you can cast them yourself. My main concern when casting is whether the student *looks* the part, as the voice will be worked on intensively throughout the play. Alternatively, you may wish to leave casting until the second session, to see who will turn up for it.

Below is an example of a rehearsal schedule which was used in a drama project based on *The Patient*, by Agatha Christie.

```
           Rehearsals for 'The Patient'

JANUARY

Monday 23: pp.9-15 - EVERYONE
Tuesday 24:  (as above)
Thursday 26: (as above)
Monday 30: pp.23-25 - EVERYONE
Tuesday 31:  (as above)

FEBRUARY

Thursday 2: pp.26-29 - Emmeline, Doctor, Inspector
Monday 6:    (as above)
Tuesday 7:pp.7-9 - Nurse, Lansen, Doctor, Inspector
Thursday 9:  (as above)
Monday 13: pp.7-15; 23-29 - EVERYONE
Tuesday 14:  (as above)
Tuesday 21: pp.29-32 - Nurse, Patient, Doctor
Thursday 23: (as above)
Monday 27: pp.7-15; 23-32 - EVERYONE
Tuesday 28: pp.16-21 - EVERYONE

MARCH

Thursday 1: pp.16-21 - EVERYONE
Saturday 3: Full Rehearsal              1.30-6 pm
Monday 5: Everything
Tuesday 6: Everything
Thursday 7: Full Dress Rehearsal
Saturday 10: Full Dress Rehearsal       1.30-6 pm
Monday 11: Full Dress Rehearsal (with video)
Thursday 14: PERFORMANCE
```

References and recommended reading

Smith, Stephen M. 1984. *The Theatre Arts and the Teaching of Second Languages*. London: Addison-Wesley.
Wagner, Betty Jane. 1979. *Dorothy Heathcote: Drama as a Learning Medium*. London: Hutchinson.

9 Rehearsals and performance

We now come to the heart of the project – rehearsals. Once you have selected your play, you need to plan your rehearsal schedule, and also decide what form each rehearsal will take. The scheme which I have outlined here is intended for a project lasting six weeks, but it can easily be adapted for longer projects. In this scheme, rehearsals take place three times a week, including the final two Saturdays before the opening night. By now, the first meeting will have taken place, the rehearsal schedule drawn up and issued to the students, help enlisted from other interested teachers, and casting more or less settled. The latter can, of course change after the first rehearsal – you may find that some students are either better suited to, or prefer, different roles. The first week is the time when any casting changes should be made, as it can be very bad for group morale and dynamics if too many changes are made later.

Scene development: an overview

If you are going to do a one-act play, divide it up into five or six coherent scenes (depending on its length). A full week's rehearsal should be allowed for each scene, but this is not a rigid rule, as some scenes are assimilated more quickly than others. The play should not be rehearsed in consecutive scenes. It is much better to start off with those scenes that require everybody to be present, in order to prevent those students who are not involved in every scene from losing interest in the project. Later you can fit in those scenes which require fewer characters. Never allow a week to go by without at least one rehearsal that requires everybody to be present. The rehearsal schedule drawn up for *The Patient* in Chapter 8 is a good example of how to handle this issue.

By the fifth week, you can start connecting the scenes and working on a smooth transition between scenes. Some of this work will already have been done in previous rehearsals, for example in that weekly rehearsal where everybody had to be present, but only now will enough ground have been covered for all the scenes to be connected.

In the fifth week, it is useful to take photographs of the students in action during rehearsals. This helps them to see what they look like to an audience, and shows whether their posture and gestures are 'in character'. If you have video-recording and filming facilities, make a video of the first dress rehearsal. You can then discuss and analyse mistakes simply by 'freezing' the scenes on the screen.

Note that if sound effects, lighting, properties, and costumes are important features of the play, they should be introduced as soon as possible (even in Week One!) to make the project more credible to the students, and also to help create the right atmosphere. Personally, I prefer plays for project work to be relatively free of paraphernalia, as this reduces costs and frees me to concentrate on the language itself.

The final week should be dedicated to full rehearsals and dress rehearsals of the whole play. The last dress rehearsal should also include practising the curtain-calls. If it is a mixed-nationality cast, it is of great interest to the audience to learn the names and nationalities of the actors, so I call on my cast to give this information to the audience themselves. Now the production is ready to be staged. Time to say: 'Break a leg!'

Early rehearsals

In the early stages of a project, when we are still familiarizing ourselves with individual scenes, I adhere fairly rigidly to the schedule outlined in Figure 15.

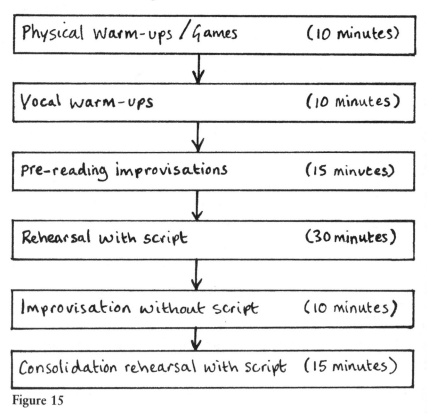

Physical warm-ups / Games	(10 minutes)
Vocal warm-ups	(10 minutes)
Pre-reading improvisations	(15 minutes)
Rehearsal with script	(30 minutes)
Improvisation without script	(10 minutes)
Consolidation rehearsal with script	(15 minutes)

Figure 15

Physical warm-ups

The rehearsals start with a variety of physical exercises to warm up the students' bodies and to break down restraint or shyness. I like to vary the exercise programme, depending on the scene I am planning to rehearse. If explosive, passionate energy is called for, the exercises will reflect this. If the scene is gentle and restrained, the exercises and games will be similar. In my experience, rehearsals without physical warm-ups lack the energy and enthusiasm of rehearsals introduced by these exercises, but if you and your group are reluctant to use them, at least start off with some games that involve running and touching, like 'Tag' discussed later in this section, or 'Cup ball' discussed in Chapter 2.

Warming up

To the basic warm-up routine, outlined in Chapter 4, some of the following exercises can be added, depending on what you wish to achieve:

- With hands clasped high above the head, bend sideways from the waist (eight times to each side). The legs should be slightly more than shoulder-width apart.
- Roll the hips eight times to the left, and eight times to the right. Keep knees slightly bent, and place hands on hips.
- Stretch up as high as possible, then flop forward so that the head and arms hang downward loosely. After relaxing in this position for a minute, slowly come up again and repeat.
- Walk around the class, changing direction frequently but taking care not to bump into anyone.

- Break into a gentle jog around the class, then gradually change to skipping.
- Jog on the spot.
- Hop from one foot to the other, and punch the air with clenched fists – forward, to the sides, and up.
- Keeping both legs together, hop from side to side.
- Vigorously shake out arms and legs at the end of the exercise routine.
- Gently massage a partner's neck and shoulders.

All the exercises are best done accompanied by pop music. Occasionally, a brisk dance can also be a great release of energy. Simply instruct the students to dance as energetically as possible.

It is very important not to overstrain their muscles during the physical warm-ups. Each participant should simply do what feels right and comfortable to him or her – it is not a competition to see who is the fittest! The exercises are followed by a few simple games which help to develop group awareness and teamwork. For example, the following games, which can all be found in Chapter 2, could be spread over the first three weeks:

Week 1: 'Cup ball', 'The statues', 'Mirrors'.

Week 2: 'The trust circle', 'Puppet on a string', 'Robot'.

Week 3: 'Concentration', 'Ear to ear', 'Watch the birdy!'.

Other games that work well are 'Tag', where one person chases all the others until she or he can touch someone else, who then becomes the chaser; 'Musical chairs', in which the group circulates around a limited number of chairs which they all try to sit on when the music stops; and 'Feelings' (see Chapter 2).

Vocal warm-ups

The next stage is warming up the students' voices. They should be pretty breathless after the physical warm-ups, so first regulate their breathing. Get them to stand in a circle and instruct them to breathe normally until their heart beats return to normal. Now practise the breathing exercises, incorporating tone and pitch, outlined in Chapter 4. This should be enough for the first rehearsal. In future rehearsals, build in some of the vocal warm-ups in Chapter 4, especially the following, which work well with any group:

papapa/bababa/tatata/dadada/kakaka/gagaga
aaaa–eeeh–aaiii–ohhh–oooh (/ɑː/ /iː/ /aɪ/ /əʊ/ /uː/)
the tip of the tongue, the teeth and the lips
minnerly/mannerly
Literary secretaries are fortunately a rarity
Whether the weather is cold/whether the weather is hot/we'll weather the weather, whatever the weather/whether we like it or not!

If the group (or any individual in the group) has particular pronunciation difficulties with any sound in English, for example the /p/ /b/ distinction for Arabic-speaking students, focus on these during the vocal warm-ups. A selection of these is given in Chapter 4. I generally end this section with a loud shout, like TOPEKA! The students' mouths and tongues are now ready for prolonged use of English.

Pre-reading improvisations

Now the actual scene-work can start. Pre-reading improvisation helps to prepare the students for the language they are about to meet in the scene to be rehearsed, and taps their already existing store of language. Here are three ways in which I have done it in the past:

1 If the scene contains specific physical activities, like building a wall, painting a picture, fighting, etc., the students are asked to present these activities through mime. At the end of the mime, they can explain it to other students in the group who were not involved in the same mime (if at all necessary).

2 The various speech acts in the scene, for example apologizing, asking permission, introducing people to each other, etc., are noted on the board, and the students are asked to produce short dialogues based on these speech acts. For example, if the scene involves introductions, ask the students to introduce people to each other, using the names of the characters in the play.

Pre-reading improvisation: Mako and Abdu mime fishing

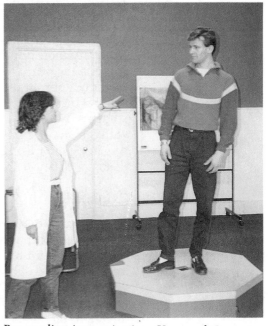

Pre-reading improvisation: Yves and Gemma improvise an argument

3 A brief synopsis of the scene is written on the board. In groups, the students work out short scenes based on it. They are allowed to observe and criticize one another's improvisations.

Naturally, you will use only one of these exercises in each rehearsal. After the vocal and physical warm-ups, improvisation of this nature comes quite readily, especially if you take an active role in it yourself.

Rehearsing with the script

Now it is time to look at the script. First read through the scene with the group, and point out particular pronunciation problems.If there are any words they do not understand, briefly explain these to them, and stress that a lot of the meaning will become clearer during the rehearsal.

Then start directing the scene, guiding the students' movements and utterances. You must have a clear idea of how and where you want them to move and perform certain gestures, but be ready to acknowledge any ideas they might have. Some directors prefer to go into rehearsals without any pre-set notions, allowing most of the ideas to come from the actors, but this can be very time-consuming and often leads nowhere. Clear, crisp leadership generally works best, especially as very few of the students will have had any acting experience. As they grow in confidence and understanding of the play, more and more ideas will come from them.

Improvisation based on the script

After carefully working through the scene with the script, ask the students to produce an improvised version of the same scene. If necessary, note down the sequence of events, together with some cues, on the board. Encourage the students to say *anything* that might be appropriate at each stage, but allow them to add bits of the script if they can remember them. Improvisation helps to free the students from over-dependence on the script, and also helps them with the actual learning of the lines. It reduces the students' fear of forgetting their lines, since they will know how to improvise some dialogue if they *do* forget.

Consolidation rehearsal with script

After the above improvisation has been completed, rehearse the scene once more, using the script. As a result of the improvisation, this should go quite smoothly, as the spontaneity and vitality of the improvisation will be added to the scene-work, thus ensuring that you end on a high note. Use the last few minutes to discuss any problems relating to the scene, and let the students write additional directions on their scripts.

Rehearsing with script in hand

Later rehearsals

By the time I start connecting the scenes, and rehearsing more than one scene per session, I dispense with most of the elements of the early rehearsals. There is no time for more than a brisk physical warm-up and a few vocal warm-ups. But once all the scenes have been rehearsed, there is normally a session in which the students can try to improvise the entire play. If they manage to do this successfully, it eases the trauma of putting away the script for the first time.

The first time that the students work without a script, you should be prepared for a very jerky, uneven presentation, full of stops and starts and repetitions, during which you will need every ounce of patience, and will constantly have to reassure them that they are doing fine. This is always the case the first time that a group works without the script, but from then on it gets much better. The fifth week is usually the time when I insist on trying out the play without the script.

The later rehearsals are best done in the room or hall where the actual performance will take place, as the students need to

A later rehearsal

familiarize themselves with their actual 'acting space', exits, entrances, and the size of the room. By now, all the essential props and other effects should have been added, so that your primary concern can be the acting.

The students should also be taught how to react when they need prompting. They should not look around frantically for the prompt (you, or another teacher), but simply hold their position and listen carefully to the prompt. Then they should just carry on as calmly as possible; giggling, clapping their hands to their mouths, or scratching their heads are not allowed! The presence of a prompt, either off-stage or on-stage, greatly reduces the stress factor, and allows them to relax and enjoy themselves.

Dress rehearsals

Treat dress rehearsals like full performances. This means insisting on silence back-stage, correct positions at the start of scenes, and full concentration. Each member of the group should be responsible for his or her outfit. If any make-up is required, enlist another teacher or non-acting student to do it. It is also useful to have a small, sympathetic audience present at these dress rehearsals, so that the students can become used to being watched and can also learn where the audience is most likely to laugh or respond in any way. This will teach them not to 'throw lines away' during audience laughter, but to wait until the laughter has subsided.

Dress rehearsal: 'Us and Them'

The first night

I usually precede my first night with an afternoon performance for the classmates and teachers of the students. This is a good preparation for the evening show, when they will perform in front of their invited guests, family, and friends. The show usually runs for two or three nights, depending on the number of people we can accommodate in the available space. After the show, the guests are offered a cup of tea and some refreshments. On some occasions in Edinburgh the show is followed by an evening of Scottish dancing.

I try to keep the atmosphere as calm and controlled as possible, unless I deliberately want to inject some tension. This I generally do if I see that the actors are over-confident and too *blasé* as a result of previous successes. I achieve the necessary degreee of tension by pointing out mistakes (exaggerating them, at times) and by giving them an extra-hard warm-up, culminating in an explosive dance. Then they are sent to their exact positions at the start of the show, and after the guests have been welcomed with a few words, the show starts.

If I am not acting myself, I control all the back-stage activities, such as sound effects, lighting, and prompting. Otherwise I enlist other students or another teacher to assist backstage. But it is better if such activities are controlled by the group that has worked together intimately for the whole period. Each student actor should take responsibility for his or her own props, and make sure that these props are in the right position *before* the audience arrives.

Naturally, the student actors should turn up a full hour before the start of the show in order to get ready. Warming up can be done after they have changed into their costumes and have set the stage. Ideally, they should go straight from warming up (done in a different room) into performance.

To publicize the shows, which are always put on free of charge, posters are put up all over the school, and the students are asked to invite their own guests to the evening shows.

Some final thoughts

It ought to be possible to produce error-free productions, if the method outlined in this chapter could be followed strictly, and if all students learned language in the same way. But what you will find is that certain learners will consistently make the same errors, in spite of all your care and attention. These are learners struggling with sentence constructions that they are not ready for, or feel uncomfortable with. As they have not yet 'acquired' a particular construction, they find difficulty in 'learning' it. The odd thing is that these students can often produce these problem sentences immediately *after* the project has ended.

Another problem that may lead to incomprehensibility is intonation. I have tried tying the intonation pattern of a particular utterance to certain gestures, in which case students find it easier to cope, and the whole group has also assisted the student with the intonation problem by chanting the utterance like a vocal warm-up. Rhythm can be reinforced by clapping out the sentence, and by marking in the pauses on the script. In fact, many of the techniques outlined in Chapter 4 can come into play during a drama project.

I have applied most of the techniques of my six-week drama projects to shorter two-week and three-week projects. Such projects are treated as dramatized playreadings: the students are not required to learn their lines, but to act while holding the script in one hand. Of course, if you are using very short sketches, they can be asked to learn their lines. So there is no reason why students on short courses, like vacation courses, cannot also benefit from drama projects. Indeed, performing a play or sketch is often the highlight of the course for such students.

Another exciting possibility, especially suitable for larger classes, is the review or variety concert. This is a combination of short sketches, mimes, improvisations, songs, choral poetry, and dance drama, which can be presented under a single theme. Such a show can absorb a large number of students, giving each one the opportunity to do a 'star turn'.

Conclusion

Thinking about my experience of drama projects, I realize that this is where my interest in the full potential of drama for language teaching first started. I wanted to transfer to my classroom the energy, motivation, discipline, creativity, and sheer enjoyment generated for my students by their involvement in drama projects. Gradually over the years I have been adding these elements to my basic classroom techniques, sometimes disastrously, but more often successfully.

The happy group

Today, drama is no longer merely a 'supplementary technique' to me, but a basic philosophy that affects every aspect of my interaction with my students. I believe in it because it changes my students from a 'roomful of strangers' into a happy, cohesive group. I believe in it because it makes the whole process of learning a language a richly creative and fulfilling experience. I believe in it because *it works*. I hope that this book will make drama work for you, too.

Bibliography

Books and papers on the theory of drama in education and language learning

Gavin Bolton *Drama as Education – An Argument for Placing Drama at the Centre of the Curriculum*. London: Longman 1984.

Frank Dunlop 'Human nature, learning and ideology.' *The British Journal of Educational Studies* XXV/3, October 1977.

Liz Johnson and **Cecily O'Neill** (eds.) *Dorothy Heathcote – Collected Writings on Education and Drama*. London: Hutchinson, 1984.

S.D. Krashen *Principles and Practice in Second Language Acquisition*. Oxford: Pergamon, 1982.

Susan Stern 'Drama in second language learning from a psycholinguistic perspective.' *Language Learning* 30/1, 1980.

Richard Via 'English through drama.' *English Teaching Forum*, July–August 1972.

Betty Jane Wagner *Dorothy Heathcote: Drama as a Learning Medium*. London: Hutchinson, 1979.

Brian Way *Development Through Drama*. London: Longman, 1967.

Teacher resource books on drama and related areas in language teaching

Suzanne Hayes *Drama as a Second Language*. Cambridge: National Extension College, 1984.

Susan Holden *Drama in Language Teaching*. London: Longman, 1981.

Alan Maley and **Alan Duff** *Drama Techniques in Language Learning*. Cambridge: Cambridge University Press, 1982.

Jane Revell *Teaching Techniques for Communicative English*. London: Allen and Unwin, 1980.

Stephen M. Smith *The Theatre Arts and the Teaching of Second Languages*. London: Addison Wesley.

Lou Spaventa (ed.) *Towards the Creative Teaching of English*. London: Allen and Unwin, 1980.

Books on theatre studies and drama workshop

Clive Barker *Theatre Games*. London: Methuen, 1977.

Peter Brook *The Empty Space*. London: Penguin, 1972. (Essential reading for anyone interested in all the elements of modern stagecraft.)

Keith Johnstone *IMPRO – Improvisation and the Theatre*. London: Methuen, 1982.

Viola Spolin *Improvisation for theTheatre*. Evanston, Illinois: North Western University Press, 1963. (Much-used classic that contains many useful exercises on improvisation; very practical.)

Constantin Stanislavsky *An Actor Prepares*. New York: Theatre Arts Books, 1936. (Ageless classic on the actor's art.)

Constantin Stanislavsky *Building a Character*. New York: Theatre Arts Books, 1949.

Susan Stanley *Drama without Script*. London: Hodder and Stoughton, 1980. (Improvisation and mime with children. Also contains many ideas suitable for adult classes.)

J. Clifford Turner *Voice and Speech in the Theatre* (revised by Morrison). London: Black 1977. (Theory and practice on the preparation of voice for the theatre.)

Sourcebooks for plays, poetry, and other texts

Collections of plays

Alan Durband (ed.) *Playbill One* (for 'Arthur' and 'Ernie's Incredible Illucinations'); *Playbill Two* (for 'The Rising Generation'); *Playbill Three*. London: Hutchinson, 1969.

John Hampden (ed.) *Twenty-four One-Act Plays* (for 'The Dear Departed' and 'The Man Who Wouldn't Go To Heaven'). London: Dent, 1979.

Mark Shackleton (ed.) *Double Act: Ten One-Act Plays on Five Themes* (for 'Over the Wall' and 'Us and Them'). London: Edward Arnold, 1985.

Peter Shaffer *Four Plays*. London: Penguin, 1981.

Stanley Richards (ed.) *Twenty One-Act Plays: An Anthology for Amateur Performing Groups* (for 'The Patient'). New York: Doubleday, 1978.

The Guide to Selecting Plays for Performance, Part 2: One-Act Plays and Revue Sketches for Mixed Casts, 84th edition. London: Samuel French.

Collections of scenes and sketches

Bits and Pieces Theatre Group *Bits and Pieces*. London: Collins, 1984.

Doug Case and **Ken Wilson** *Off-Stage!* and *Further Off-Stage!*. London: Heinemann, 1978/1985.

John McRae *Using Drama in the Classroom*. Oxford: Pergamon, 1985.

M. Schulman and **E. Meckler** *Contemporary Scenes for Student Actors*. New York: Penguin, 1980.

Poetry and prose

M. Benton and **P. Benton** *Touchstones*. London: Hodder and Stoughton, 1971.

P. Brendon and **W. Shaw** (eds.) *Readings They've Liked*. London: Macmillan, 1967. (Combines poetry and prose.)

Circus of Poets *OK Gimme – Poems for Children*. Rotherham: Versewagon Press, 1985.

James Gibson (ed.) *Let the Poet Choose*. London: Harrap, 1975.

Alan Maley and **Sandra Moulding** *Poem Into Poem*. Cambridge: Cambridge University Press, 1984.

Piers Plowright *Read English*. London: Heinemann, 1973.

Geoffrey Summerfield (ed.) *Voices – the Third Book*. London: Penguin 1968.

John Turner *Hard Shoulders Second Home*. Rotherham: Versewagon, 1984.

Role plays (mainly written as open-ended sketches)

Marion Gow *The Commercial Scene – Role-playing for Commerce Students*. London: Edward Arnold, 1982.

Richard Nicholson *Open to Question – Starters for Discussion and Role-play*. London: Edward Arnold, 1978.

David Walker *Dilemmas 1, 2, and 3*. London: Edward Arnold, 1979/1982/1983.

David Walker *Kith and Kin*. London: Edward Arnold, 1981.

Sourcebooks in language teaching using drama and related activities

M. Christison and **S.Bassano** *Look Who's Talking*. Oxford: Pergamon, 1981. (A variety of communication activities for language learners.)

J. Dixey and **M. Rinvolucri** *Get Up and Do It!* London: Longman, 1978. (Sketches, mimes, and role plays for EFL.)

Marion Geddes and **Gill Sturtridge** *Video in the Language Classroom*. Practical Language Teaching series. London: Heinemann, 1982. (See Chapter 6 for 'Student video production' by Elayne Phillips.)

Carolyn Graham *Jazz Chants*. New York: Oxford University Press, 1978. (An invaluable and widely-used aid for the teaching of rhythm.)

J. Heyworth *The Language of Discussion*. London: Hodder and Stoughton, 1979. (Reading, discussion, and role play; essential language provided to accompany role plays.)

Alan Maley, Alan Duff, and **Françoise Grellet** *The Mind's Eye*. Cambridge: Cambridge University Press, 1980. (Pictures as a stimulus to discussion and role play.)

John Morgan and **Mario Rinvolucri** *Once Upon A Time*. Cambridge: Cambridge University Press, 1983. (The use of story telling in language teaching.)

C. Mortimer. *Dramatic Monologues for Listening Comprehension*. Cambridge: Cambridge University Press, 1980. (Can be extended for improvisation; excellent for intonation practice.)

Gillian Porter Ladousse *Role Play*. Oxford: Oxford University Press, 1987. Part of the 'Resource Books for Teachers' Series.

Gillian Porter Ladousse *Speaking Personally*. Cambridge: Cambridge University Press, 1983. (Personal questionnaires, discussion and role-play activities.)

Mario Rinvolucri *Grammar Games*. Cambridge: Cambridge University Press, 1984. (Includes drama games.)

E. Romijn and **C. Seely** *Live Action English*. Oxford: Pergamon, 1981. (Using the Total Physical Response in teaching beginners and elementary learners.)

Peter Watcyn-Jones *Act English*. London: Penguin, 1978. (Twenty-five excellent role plays.)

Megan Webster and **Libby Castañon** *Crosstalk 1, 2, and 3*. Oxford: Oxford University Press, 1980. (Role-play and other communication activities, ranging from elementary to upper-intermediate level.)

Andrew Wright, David Betteridge, and **Michael Buckley** *Games for Language Learning*. Cambridge: Cambridge University Press, 1979. (A wide variety of language games.)